Dorothy McRa

Being Clergy, Staying Human

taking our stand in the river

an alban institute publication

The Publications Program of The Alban Institute is assisted by a grant from Trinity Church, New York City.

Library of Congress Catalog Card #92-72457.
ISBN 1-56699-056-4.

CONTENTS

FOREWORD

Perhaps the most difficult task for parish clergy is getting some perspective on their role in the church and beyond the church in the larger community. No human condition is outside the clergy's responsibility. Every hurt, failure, and disappointment calls out for healing. Every hope, success, and strength yearns for confirmation. Only a person who has the freedom and ability to stand far enough away to see the masses but close enough to feel the pain of each person can fill this role with confidence and accomplishment.

I would like for Dorothy McRae-McMahon to be my pastor. She has that uncommon gift of reflecting thoughtfully and continually on the church's ministry, on her role as a pastor, and on how her people live and grow and serve. She has the insight for teaching, guiding, leading, and supporting people over the rapids and through the eddies of the river. Even in the reading of this book, we are led and nurtured.

Being Clergy, Staying Human is an autobiographical account of ministry in Dorothy's parish. The focus is less on her role as pastor and more on how her role reflects commitment and humanness, honesty and faithfulness, vulnerability and courage, forgiveness and healing, weakness and authenticity among all the people who seek God in that place. It is a moving story of people being loved and loving, being healed and healing.

Dorothy shows how worship, liturgy, preaching, pastoral care, and prophetic engagement can encourage and assist people to deal with pain, disappointment, and brokenness. She also shows how thoughtful, purposeful leadership can enable people to encourage and assist others.

I invite clergy who need perspective and new evidence of the possibilities for non-anxious ministry to wade in with Joshua, the priests of Israel, and Dorothy. Dorothy is a good pastor and leader. Those of us who walk with her for a while will be too!

Ezra Earl Jones
General Secretary
The General Board of Discipleship
The United Methodist Church

INTRODUCTION

When the people of Israel were waiting on the banks of the Jordan River to enter the Promised Land, God told Joshua to tell the priests: "Lift up the Ark of the Covenant and pass in front of the people . . . Tell them that when they come to the edge of the waters of the Jordan, they are to take their stand in the river" (Josh. 3:6, 8).

This has always been, for me, a vivid image of the role of the clergy. I picture the people of God in every age receiving with hope and faith the dream of a new heaven and a new earth. I see the people waiting and watching for the ones among them who will take hold of that dream and step into the river of life, the ones who will tell them what it feels like in the river and demonstrate what they need to carry with them if they are to live in that river with faith, integrity, and a sense of adventure.

In this small book I will reflect on some of the things I have learned as I have walked into the river of life with the people and staff colleagues of the Pitt Street Uniting Church in the center of the city of Sydney, Australia, and to a lesser degree with the people of Palmer Street Church in nearby Darlinghurst. For nearly a decade the people of the Pitt Street church have taught me what the clergy ministry is as they called forth from me the modest gifts I have had to offer. They have loved me through all my trials and errors and shared their lives with me in trust and hope. Together we have continued the renewal of the life of our congregation. Most of this book is our story.

I have pondered long and often about what it might mean to take the stand in the river ahead of the people, and, in trying to live out my understandings, I have moved from a heroic view to one of costly humanness. As I have stood in the river, I have found that the rich company of the laity has given me endless encouragement and expanding clarity, so that being first to step into the river loses its terrors. The journey becomes rather a great celebration of the passion of the life to which we are called and a powerful recognition of the God in Christ who places the firm rock under our feet, holds out the steadying branches for us to grab, sweeps us on past the rapids, and carries us gently on the current.

CHAPTER I

Standing in the River of True Humanness

As we prepare to enter the ordained ministry, it is easy to think that the clergy role is about being called to heroism. As the preparation unfolds, we see ourselves as expert theologians, biblical scholars, ethicists, counselors, therapists, administrators, educators, facilitators of groups, liturgists, preachers, church historians, philosophers, and community organizers. Then throw in a bit of prophecy and fund raising.

But things can quickly get even more complicated. Many professions require extensive preparation but few overlay powerful pressure on their members to be "special" people—people who are "icons" of morality, who never doubt or are confused about life, who cope with everything and everybody with peaceful competence.

Few people are called to live their private lives within their public professions, and few are expected to be publicly accountable for the private lives of their whole families.

Given all this, I watch many clergy colleagues, and sometimes myself, being caught in a dreadful rhythm: on the one hand trying to "up" our performance with more study and more professional workshops; on the other hand taking more retreats and stress-management courses in an effort to keep ourselves together.

I ask myself, "Is this what it means to take our stand in the river ahead of the people?"

The Clergy as Perceived by Others

Perhaps because I was a layperson for most of my life and a clergyperson's daughter, I have experienced, often with pain, the way clergy are perceived by other people. I remember planning speakers for the key nights of a parish mission. When we came to the big event to which we were inviting the public, someone said, "We'll need to have a layperson for this night because clergy don't know about real life."

I also watch, with some anguish and some awareness of truth, the portrayal of clergy in literature and the media. I see mostly three images: the stupid, wimpish, pathetic person who is regarded as a joke; the austere cloistered person who is quite irrelevant to life; and the self-righteous, authoritarian person who is caught in sexual immorality. Occasionally we are treated to the rather lovable, usually hard-drinking, jolly Catholic priest.

I also see the way many people's behavior changes when they find out that I am a person "of the cloth" (whatever that means!). They immediately put their guard up and assume that I will be shocked by or disapproving of ordinary human behavior. I find myself wanting to shout, "How dare you assume I am not human like you are?" or to swear a little at the first opportunity to prove that I am a human being. I always have to work extra hard in relationships to prove that I am not "delicate," overly good, or particularly self-righteous.

The irony is that, while all this is going on in social relationships, most of us are relating day after day to people in trauma who assume that we can handle the murkiest and most painful aspects of life! Such desperate people tend to put us in the role of God figures who are their last hope rather than human beings who would deeply understand.

When I reflect on these relationships, I ask myself, "Do these people really see me as a likely person to accompany them into the river of life, let alone lead them into the river?" It's rough trying to live heroically when the lifestyle in effect separates you from the supports inherent in being seen as part of the human race.

Leading the Way into Humanness

What would it really be like to be perceived by others as the one who is prepared to step into the river of life first—ahead of them?

I think the time has come to lay aside the saint and martyr images, which are largely oppressive and unattractive, and to dare to lead the way into authentic humanness. If we need the witness of Jesus Christ before us, I believe we have it. Jesus appears to have been a rigorous and human figure. He was indeed a good man but the Scriptures do not present him as saintly in an otherworldly sense. He was tired. He was sometimes ragingly angry. He obviously associated with ordinary, interesting sinners of various types. We put him down if we imply that he was their friend simply to save them; I think he liked them! I doubt that he planned to die; sometimes, if you live fully, you have to be killed. He gave the impression of choosing his life rather than responding to expectations and pressures.

I remember a most vivid experience of "transfiguration" when I stood in the Sistine Chapel in Rome and looked up at Michelangelo's Jesus—leaping off the wall, full of muscle, passion, and vigor. No one would doubt that such a Jesus was real and human. I felt connected in a powerful way with the real witness of the life and death of Jesus and just as powerfully alienated from the traditional images for clergy who are called to represent that Christ.

"And so," I ask myself, "could it be that the bravest and truest way to lead people into life is to be authentically human ourselves?" What is the worst thing that could happen if we stopped being "special"? I suppose that some of us would lose our parishes, because we have created churches made up of members who demand a dehumanized clergy. But maybe we could act together and support one another so that we create a more human church.

Experience has shown me that the world is waiting for a human church—where people can be honest with one another, in which leaders give clear evidence of going through universal human struggles. We might lose a few tyrannical people on the way and possibly some money, but what freedom we would have!

Signs of a Rehumanized Clergy Ministry

The clearest sign of a humanized clergy is our feeling free to tell the truth. An example? When they say (whoever "they" are), "You ought to be doing such and such," we should feel free to say, "I can't because I am too tired," or "I would rather not do that because I am not good at doing it. Can't one of you do it?" In another context we could admit, with regret, "I'm sorry. I messed that up," or "I forgot," without feeling as if we were betraying our calling.

Obviously no church boards will appreciate gross incompetence for long, but that is not what I am proposing. We all know that most of us feel in jeopardy if we confess to the most modest inadequacies. We expect to teach people convincingly about the grace of God without giving them real opportunities to be gracious to us. We expect people to believe in the grace of God without bearing witness to our own daily experience of grace.

Some of the highest moments in my ministry have come when I have been prepared to receive the grace of the lay leaders in the parish. To reflect openly on one's own struggle to find the resources to live a life of faith gives others permission to do the same. It gives others the opportunity to offer us their resources; at the very least, it lowers the pressures on us all so that we may survive together until new energy arises.

Early in my ordained ministry I received a request from a particular nationwide group for permission to hold on the front steps of our church a hunger strike (to the death) in defense of their current struggle. I took the request to the church board and we all sat in rather tense silence before beginning a "clever" discussion: Do we know enough about the cause these people are fighting for? Do we think hunger strikes are theologically and idealogically sound? Then a very honest and earthy person among us said, "Well, bloody hell, I don't want them dying on our front steps when the state governor comes to our 150th anniversary service!" We all laughed with relief and confessed that for worthy and unworthy reasons we couldn't cope with supporting this initiative. We took it into our next worship service and named ourselves before God as people who weren't always able to live up to our own hopes for ourselves.

We lost nothing in that confession. On the contrary, I—and we—learned a great deal about the creative power of honest response and the relief of rediscovering our common humanity. It didn't mean that we were sliding down a slippery slope, eager to wriggle out of any difficult situation. It taught us that, if we were real with one another, we could be open to any initiative and, in the presence of an infinitely kind God, sometimes admit our frailty and sometimes find astonishing new courage and energy together.

One of the harder areas for me is being honest when I don't know something. Probably because I don't have a good memory for detail, I have developed great techniques for covering when I don't know or don't remember something. I don't actually lie; I just imply things! I have a strong inner need to be the one who "knows" things—not just the answers to questions but inside information about people and situations. It is easy to give the impression of being important if we seem to know all the inside information. It also confirms our expert status if we make people believe that we always know things about theology and the Bible. I mean, what's the use of paying for trained clergy if they don't know things?

Clearly, again, there is a difference between simple honesty and incompetence. To say that we will need to research something or defer to a colleague is to communicate that we are comfortable with our fallibility—that we have no need to fear our ordinary human ignorances and no need to compete with more well informed people.

People are extraordinarily astute in telling the difference between those who are securely grounded in life and faith and those who pretend to be. If they recognize the solid base—firmly set in our own security—our ongoing searchings encourage them in theirs. They know full well that mature faith is not built on an absence of doubt.

I find the most difficult area in which to be vulnerable is in what would normally be regarded as one's private life. Even if we are committed to vulnerable humanness, the nature of the clergy role raises questions in this area. I believe that church members should not be encouraged to think that they have any right to make judgments on the lifestyle and/or state of being of any of the family of the clergyperson. Genuine concern for their well-being may be appropriate, given the time and energy pressure under which most clergy work. We should all try to move away from the "model Christian family" expectation that has prevailed. Relationships are very complex, and we as clergy need to set the standards in relation to interpreting another's relationships by refusing to let simplistic judgments be made of our own. We all know that the most conscientious parents can have children with messy lives and that couples who begin a marriage relationship faithfully can still end up in trouble.

Yet there is a fine line between the trusting sharing of the human struggle and an inappropriate and unhealthy need for self-disclosure of one's private life.

To share with dignity that you are having difficulties and are seeking help is honest, trusting, and usually reassuring. It alerts the sisters and brothers to the fact that you need their concern and prayer without enmeshing them in the details of the problems or their solutions. It also signals that you are acting responsibly in attempting to get appropriate counsel and help rather than being paralyzed in personal chaos.

Frank openness may be helpful to the ongoing life of the parish in situations where it is not a matter of "trouble" in the straightforward sense. Let's say your children decide to live in a defacto marriage relationship and you are aware that many parishioners are troubled by the same situation with their own children. You might be the first to risk a creative "stepping into the river of vulnerability." Where fear of one another's judgments brings on silence around a common concern, clergy are, I believe, called to give the lead.

By giving the lead, we can often determine the way the reflection will go. For example, if we say "My children are living in sin. How can I stop them?", the discussion is likely to heap punishment on everyone. Of course, people who feel this way are not likely to bring up the topic, fearing that the punishment of the community of faith will be added to their own and presumably God's punishment of them as "bad" parents.

If, on the other hand, we say "My children have decided to live with their partners without being married. I'm not sure how to think about that because I love and respect them and I can see that they are very committed and faithful to their partners. But I married, and I guess I always hoped that my children would do the same. How do other people grapple with the situation? How do we understand Christian values and ethics in this area today?" When we do this, we invite other people to expose their own concerns and reflect painfully but gently with one another.

Obviously, if there is a major change in your life, such as a marital breakdown, you have no option but to be honest. As my own marriage ended, I feared that such a massive failure would seriously threaten my ministry. As I took the leap, I felt as though I was about to jump off a cliff into a bottomless pit. I remember standing before God and saying, "Dear God, I can do no other. I have nothing left but dependence on your grace and a very fragile faith that your love will be waiting for me somewhere." I ended the marriage, told my elders' council, and entered an experience of such love and grace that every day since has been a thanksgiving. I knew to the depths of my soul what it meant to be saved by grace through faith.

I also learned that the people of God can surround their clergy with loving forgiveness as my parishioners gathered up in their care both myself and my ex-husband. Even though there were a few weeks when I could hardly get through the sermon—mainly because of the loving eyes upon me—my competence for ministry was never in question. If anything, it expanded as people recognized my humanness and received my thankful witness to grace and to the capacity of the community of faith to give loving acceptance and support in human failure and ambiguity.

Entering the River

Maybe we are, in the end, called to a particular sort of courage. It may be heroic to endure many things and never share our suffering, our fear of failing, our exhaustion, or our doubts. I suspect it takes more courage to be real with people, especially people in the church of today. If we will not be real, we participate in the maintaining of churches that will never be truly inviting to real people, churches that support only the "successful," where all people are "faithful," all are "coping," and all are, in the end, afraid of being "found out."

If we will not bear witness to the beauty of humanness, how will people ever believe that Christ has come among them? If we will not let ourselves be loved as we really are, how will the people believe that they can be loved by us, one another, and God when their "secrets" are revealed? They will not trust the church; they will instead take their realities to therapists, doctors, and hairdressers. They will blot out their realities with drugs and alcohol.

In our parish we have found that it is possible to create a relatively honest community of faith. We don't pretend to sustain that all of the time with all of the people, but when we do image that hope and try to live it out, people bring their friends to join us. They see that we are just an ordinary "bunch of sinners" doing our best to accompany one another on the journey of life and giving thanks for a gracious God. As the one who steps into the river first, I know I have a grave responsibility to give the sort of leadership that consistently reinstates the human.

As we try to hold to this together, people know that their human pain will not be devalued—that when life seems unjust, we will weep together and cry out to God as the psalmists had the confidence to do.

As I have dared to step into the river of humanness first, I have gained, not lost, credibility. I still work very hard, but I am not doing so to live up to anyone else's expectations. I do it with a grateful heart because I love my work (most of the time!). I might get tired, but I don't become stressed as often as I once did. That's because I have reduced the pretences and the lies to myself and other people, and this has reduced my fear.

Do they crucify you if you are vulnerable? Yes, sometimes. In my experience, those who criticize you most are clergy colleagues who are trapped in their own fear of vulnerability. Or some see a relaxed style of ministry that flows along in a stream of love, which they envy and resent. But once you step into the river of humanness, I can't imagine you would want to go back to the desert of apparent invulnerability for too long; it is too lonely, too alienating from one's own self, too far from a kindly God, and too pale a shadow of the rigor of real life.

Living vulnerably in leadership opens you to pain in many ways, but pain is usually an opportunity to grow, to discover life out of death. As you walk through pain, it does not hurt any less, but it teaches you that you can survive. It becomes a liturgy of survival memories. It becomes part of the rich and strong fabric of life. It strips your faith back to the certain rock of the grace of God, the life-giving power of Jesus Christ and the miracles of the Holy Spirit.

You begin to become like the wise old Skin Horse in Margery Williams's beautiful story *The Velveteen Rabbit*. In the story the Rabbit was asking the Skin Horse how one became real. The Skin Horse talked about being loved for a long time and how becoming real was a long process.

He said, "You become . . . That's why it doesn't often happen to people who break easily, or have sharp edges, or who have to be carefully kept. Generally by the time you are Real, most of your hair has been loved off, your eyes drop out and you get very shabby."

He said that these things don't matter at all once your are Real—they only matter to people who don't understand.

The Rabbit decided it would be a long time before he became Real and wished that it could happen without his being so uncomfortable.*

* Margery Williams, *The Velveteen Rabbit* (Transworld Publishers Ltd., Ealing London, 1980. First published by William Heinemann Ltd., 1922.)

CHAPTER II

Lifting Up the Ark

We are the people who are called to lift up the "ark of the covenant" for the people—to hold it high above the threatening floods of life, to cherish and protect it in harsh times. This is our sacred task. But sometimes the community of faith has lost the wonder of its sacramental life; it is taken for granted or not really understood; it has become an empty ritual.

If their power is to be claimed, long-standing rituals often need to be refreshed. While the celebration of the Eucharist may be important in the life of a church community, people may not be aware of its power as a personal, spiritual resource. One of the ways our parish has revitalized the gift of the Eucharist is by carrying it out of the church building to groups that see themselves as marginal and unworthy. Of course this is not done lightly. It comes after relationships have been established and there is a growing sense of community. Often it happens when the group, a mixture of members of the parish and the marginalized group, have been eating together for a while, developing a sense of solidarity. It seems a very natural thing to introduce the central sustaining sacrament of the life of the church into, for example, the normal shared meal of the community. It then becomes for those people, in the most vivid fashion, a Eucharistic meal. It is particularly powerful to raise the bread among a rejected group within a community and say, "On the night he was betrayed . . ." Almost always the presence of the Christ is powerfully evident when the marginalized group receives with wonder the solemn gift offered to them without conditions. The church members, who may well have been taking such a gift for granted, suddenly realize that they have something infinitely precious in their hands.

They often go back to the chruch community exuding the spirit of the early disciples who said they had seen the Christ. On the other hand, the marginalized group has received a deep insight into the center of faith and hope of the Christian community.

There was once a thought that when dealing with a deprived group of people worship and sacraments should be kept simple and plain—no robes, very informal, no candles. But the poor are used to being given everything without frills. When we carry the "ark" to them, we should remember that they deserve everything we can bring them in all its drama, color, and beauty. After all, they are invited to the feast of heaven.

The Eucharist as a Rite of Healing and Forgiveness

Most clergy have had people come to them and say, in effect, "I have been to two psychiatrists, three therapists, and several other counselors. I know why I am and who I am, but I can't seem to move on."

This scenario can push us into asking ourselves if the church actually has a unique role in healing and forgiving. Why do we not seize boldly the most powerful things we have and offer them? The Roman Catholic Church has long recognized the power of rituals for forgiveness and healing. Protestants are often wary of introducing practices that may become superstitious or meaningless, repetitious acts. But why not explore what could happen if we work with the theology of such rites and use them carefully and sparingly?

We have held such services, with appropriate variations, for people needing reconciliation with God at the ending of a marriage. Obviously the focus depends on the particular issue confronting the person concerned; sometimes the person initiating the divorce cannot experience forgiveness; sometimes it is both people mutually wishing to mark the ending of the relationship; sometimes it is one partner wishing to be healed of the deep hurt.

We have also held services for people facing situations that can no longer be directly resolved. Maybe an abusing parent has died without giving any recognition to the harm that has been done to the child, now adult. We gather around the offended person and hear the story of the relationship. The person reads a list of positive and negative memories of the relationship and shows good and bad symbols of the experience. As we share the grief, we look at everything with honesty. In the liturgy we name the pain, the betrayals, the laughter, and the survivals. We commemorate leaving behind the negative, and we celebrate the good. We place flowers around a photo of the parent and lay hands on the child for healing. We carry out an act of farewell, laying the parent to rest, and we affirm the future.

We will soon have a service for a young woman who was sexually assaulted by her priest some time ago. We are planning a representative confession by the church, which betrayed a sacred trust. We will tell the story and grieve for her wounding. We will pass around a bowl of salt water and taste the tears of all who have been betrayed by the church. We will have an anointing and laying on of hands for her healing and share a Eucharist with a special focus on the betrayal of Christ and the hope of the resurrection.

Services like this are always conducted in a lovingly prepared environment that includes signs that the person is being cherished— flowers, music, and candles. A small number of carefully chosen companions for the journey stand by.

Ritualizing such occasions "honors" the special moment when one publicly chooses in faith to be healed. The ritual often stops the endless searching for resolution, forgiveness, and healing and brings the person to peace.

If we see a service of forgiveness or healing as a carefully constructed liturgy of prayer and sacrament that creates a special "survival memory" for at least one person and as a respectful waiting on the gift of God, many wonderful things can happen.

The following is an example of a service for forgiveness and restoration.

SERVICE OF FORGIVENESS AND HEALING

The Witness

Leader: *In Jesus Christ we hear the Good News*
              that God is like a mother hen
              who shelters her chickens under her warm wings.

People: *We believe that God is love.*

Leader: *In Jesus we see a God*
             who weeps for the people of the world.

People: *And weeps for our wounding.*

Leader: *In Jesus we see a God*
             who reaches out with healing hands

People: *Who sees our pain and makes us whole.*

Confession

Leader: *Loving God,*
             when we fail we face an experience of death:
             the death of an image we had of ourselves,
             a death of a hope about ourselves,
             a death of a relationship that we wished to value.
             We wonder whether we were wrong in our beginnings
             or wrong in our endings.
             We experience your absence
             as we hide our faces from you.

             We come into your presence now
             believing that we have faced things
             that were too great for us.
             We come before you
             and confess that we have failed.
             We have wounded ourselves and those we love.
             Our faith in our own worth and beauty is shaken.

People: *Forgive us, O God.*

Leader: *In our brokenness,*
             we need your healing and recreating,
             your power to restore us to
             the hope of fullness of life.

People: *Forgive us, O God.*

Leader: *In the silence, we make our own confession to you.*
[silent prayer]
Forgive us, O God.

People: *Forgive us and help us, O God.*

Assurance of Pardon

[The person concerned kneels and is surrounded by the people]

Leader: *To God, our endings can be the beginnings.*
Our deaths can be the road to resurrection.
We bear the consequences for what we do,
but we are not condemned.

Receive the gift of new life
and the sign that, even at this moment,
you are one with Christ
who will never leave you nor forsake you
to the end of time.

[laying on of hands and anointing]

Go in peace, free forever from all that has gone before.
In the name of God the Creator, God the Redeemer, and
God the Sustainer.

This is followed by Bible readings, a brief homily, special prayers of intercession for the person concerned (preferably by various supportive friends), and prayers for all those who labor under guilt.

If appropriate, those gathered can celebrate the Eucharist. We serve the wine in a new pottery chalice, and after everyone in the circle of communion has received from this common cup, the clergyperson places the chalice in the hands of the person being healed and says:

Take this cup.
It is a common cup, and we give it to you
as a reminder of our common humanness.
Your life is a part of our life and,
in our common brokenness,

we are all dependent on the grace of God.
Keep it as a sign that you are forgiven
and free to live again in faith, hope, and love.
Remember that we shared this common cup with you.

A service like this has the capacity to move the person beyond working out his or her own destiny. The person can take any good work that has been done with a therapist and place it in the hands of God and the community of faith to be carried in faith beyond self-healing and forgiveness. The service teaches people that we can always go further than we thought we could because resources are available that are beyond our own energy or deserving. Such a service also teaches us to live corporately—that we are not meant to live alone and find everything from within ourselves.

People usually value the small chalice they have been given, not as a "magic" article but as a reminder of a particular moment of community that encourages them to trust that they are never alone and always loved by God.

The Enhancing of Baptism

The beautiful sacrament of Baptism is, of course, complete in itself; who would question its profound and total message of grace? But it can take on a new relevance as an initiation ceremony when we compliment it with small acts that arise from the life of a particular congregation.

For example, our congregation sensed that it would like both to receive an insight from the indigenous people of Australia and to reflect our commitment to be people who try to live out an incarnate faith. So, as we baptize our children, we place their feet in a bowl of earth, recognizing the Aboriginal insight that the earth is our mother; we invite parents to join us in teaching the child that the earth is a place in which we are working with God for justice, peace, and freedom for the whole creation.

Then, after the baptism, we carry the baptized child into our high pulpit (one of the few times we use it!), and we show the child the congregation and say, "This church belongs to you and these are your people. They are yours in their beauty and yours in their humanness."

We then say a prayer for the particular child, affirming the personality characteristics that we already see present, maybe peacefulness, lively joy, energy, or openness. We show the child the great text painted over the arch of our sanctuary, and we say, "Over the life of this church lies a great text from Holy Scripture: Where the Spirit of the Lord is, there is liberty. We give that Word to you to carry with you for the rest of your life."

As we do these things, we feel as though we are gaining a sense of our own special community and creating a proud tradition.

The Eucharist as Community

By its very nature, the service of Holy Communion should be an experience of community at the very deepest level. But if we have always served communion with people individually choosing to come forward by themselves to a communion rail or to a serving station, we have reduced the communal experience of the sacrament. If we go back to the sacramental roots in the action of Jesus serving his friends around a table, we can imagine a very intimate experience. While that sort of experience cannot always be reproduced in a modern church setting and our different practices of distribution may well have become precious to us, it is important to ask ourselves whether our people know more about community at the end of the Eucharist than they did at the beginning.

Breaking through into a different experience of distribution, even occasionally, can restore a freshness of the power of sacramental community. Asking people to form a large circle around the aisles of the church and serve one another or be served as they look at other faces can remind us that we are one in Christ. Singing quietly together as we are served is a uniting act. Asking people as they are served to gather others into the communion—loved ones who are absent or particular suffering peoples from around the world—reminds us that we are a communion encompassing more than those present. You might have members of the congregation or worship leaders name different struggling groups from around the world; after each naming sing something like the Taize chant, "Jesus remember them when you come into your kingdom." This can create a moving sense of community with one another and with the Christ who is present in the bread and wine.

More frequent incorporation of the Eucharist into significant communal parish meals can also enhance the understanding of the eucharistic community to which we belong.

The Rhythm of Worship As the Rhythm of Life

Lay people who are invited to work with clergy in the preparation of worship often recognize that the traditional "shape" of liturgy—the approach, confession, absolution, affirmation of faith, intercession, blessing, and sending out—reflects a creative rhythm for the whole of one's spiritual life. I am not implying that one must introduce a set spiritual discipline into each day. Rather, I am recognizing that people who are healthily facing reality—engaging with it and moving and growing in response to it—can see in that process an echo of the liturgy. Once they see this, worship takes on new meaning and life involves a more intentional and personal pattern of communion with God. They move beyond the you-must-read-your-Bible-and-pray-every-day-or-feel-guilty stage of spirituality.

You might invite people to remember some period of personal change, growth, or survival. Looking back, what patterns or stages can they identify? At an early point they may have been aware of the possibility of newness, of God, of something beyond where they were; or at least they felt a longing for something beyond them. I see this as *the approach*. They may recall staying in that mode for some time.

They may describe a concurrent or subsequent response as being conscious of how far removed they were from the dream, from the life of God. They may have stayed with this *Confessional* period for some time, too.

Then they may recall what moved them from that paralysis of inadequacy or guilt. They may remember what became the *absolution* or the *Word* for them at that time.

So what did they do? Did they in effect *affirm their faith*: "I believe that I have a new power to move or change or survive?"

Did they ask for help to do that from God or their friends (*intercession*)?

Did they prepare for the moment of change with some ritual of support—sharing a meal or drink with someone, giving themselves a small encouraging gift, writing down their commitment to move, telling someone else they were going to make the change (*moment of agape or eucharist or blessing*)?

Did they finally gather themselves together, take a deep breath, and act (*the sending out*)?

Obviously not everybody can identify moments as neatly as this, but most people can recognize some such pattern. As worship leader, you can help people see this as a God-intended pattern of healthy life, a pattern that it is best lived in community with others, just as worship is lived out in community.

Congregations in traditions that offer the chance to create new liturgies can be set free to create wonderfully imaginative worship if they understand and appreciate the theology of it in the first place.

With this new understanding, congregations in traditions that have more or less set liturgies can consider all sorts of symbolic acts—additions of art, drama, dance, and poetry—that will enhance and deepen the liturgy's relevance and meaning. For example, seeing confession as a moment of weakness, of awareness of who one is, rather than as a moment of guilt, might lead to the introduction of symbols that say, "This is who we are, God." Such a new twist can take confession beyond a repetition of words.

Bridging into the Community outside the Church

Let me relate two incidents when we as a parish were able to carry the "ark" into the world.

On the first occasion we were under attack by a neo-Nazi group that had been harassing us because of our stand against racism. After a long period of this, which had become public knowledge, we decided to take the initiative. We invited the community at large to share with us in a liturgical celebration of the unity of all humankind. We used the normal pattern of liturgy but without religious language. This is the liturgy we developed:

A CELEBRATION OF THE UNITY OF ALL HUMANKIND

Informal Greeting

Naming Our Meeting

Leader: *Many traditions and many cultures are ours.*

People: *We stand among each other*
               with different histories and beliefs.

Leader: *A common earth and an essential kinship*
               are also ours.

People: *We stand among each other.*
               We share our planet.
               We share birth, death, hunger, and love.

Leader: *Let us celebrate our unity:*

People: *Our love unites us.*
               Our struggles unite us.
               We seek joy in many ways.
               We are human together
               in our ambiguity, our fear, and our hope.

[The people sit.]

Naming our Separation

Leader: *Even as we name our meeting,*
               we face the things that separate us:
               Injustice [silent reflection]
               Racism [silent reflection]
               Prejudice [silent reflection]
               Violence [silent rejection]

Choir [Taize chant]

               "By night we travel in darkness
               with only a thirst to guide us."

Leader: *Into fear:*

People: *Breathe wonder.*

Leader: *Into anger:*

People: *Breathe trust.*

Leader: *Into defense:*

People: *Breathe tenderness.*

Leader: *Into oppressions:*

People: *Breathe freedom.*

Leader: *Into dividedness:*

People: *Breathe love.*

Leader: *Let us rise up and live with hope.*

Stories of Human Unity

[Community leaders tell personal experiences—moments of human unity.]

[After each story the people sing the following response by D. B. Pill:]

> *Moment of unity, gift of forgiveness,*
> *fountain of freedom, promises of newness.**

Celebrating Unity in Diversity

Leader: *All people are the people of the light.*
              Let us celebrate our unity in diversity.
              [Symbols of ethnic diversity are placed by each person on
              the table.]

*Copyright 1972 words: Rev. D. B. Pill, music: Peter Waters, Rodan Publications, Adelaide, Australia.

Representatives of ethnic groups:
> *I offer the gifts of the _____ community into our life.*

People:
> *We celebrate the gifts of the _____ community in our life together.*

Representative of indigenous people:
> *The gifts of my people have always waited here.*
> *They will be released by justice.*

People:
> *We celebrate the hope of justice and reconciliation for us all.*

Song for Peace [sung by choir or solo]

Affirmation of Unity

Leader:
> *Beside each other, within the earth,*
> *we are in her and of her,*
> *are vulnerable with her,*
> *are her people.*

People:
> *Father sky opens above us and we receive space.*
> *Mother earth stands beneath us and we receive ground.*
> *Sister air becomes our breath and we are one wind.*
> *Brother water becomes our blood and we are one sea.*
> *Living things die for us.*
> *And we die, returning to soil, sea, and air.*

Leader:
> *We are the people of pain and fear.*
> *We are the people of anger and joy.*
> *We are the people of compassion and grace.*

People:
> *We are each of us this.*
> *We are all of us this.*
> *We name our own God.*
> *We are one.*

Leader:
> *In all of us is a longing*

> *for a life that has not yet come,*
> *for a world that is free and just,*
> *a dream of hope for all people.*

Community song

Sending Out

Leader: *Go from here*
and take with you the unity of this night.
Go strong in the hope that lies in our shared humanity,
committed to the struggle for a new day
and claiming the courage and truth
that stands beyond and between us,
however you name that reality.
Go in peace.

Many people came to the deeply moving service and saw that in that symbolic act we were trying to model the relationships we could live out together. They were grateful that we assumed that the wider community might want to join with us in celebrating the dream of human community. They were grateful that the church had offered its understanding of creative rituals for life to the whole community without "strings" or conditions.

At the celebration of unity in diversity, about six representatives of ethnic groups came forward, as prearranged. After they had spoken, we asked if anyone else would like to offer his or her particular ethnicity into the community, and nearly sixty people did so. As I said, this was a deeply moving and emotional service.

I recall another occasion when we took our liturgy into the community. This time I was approached by a small group of women from a community under attack by a rapist who had not been caught. Community life was breaking down as more than fifty women had been raped in a variety of circumstances, at all times of day. Women were afraid to go anywhere, afraid in their own homes, and unable to trust the men of the community. In response to their request, we invited all the women of the little township to come for a "Gathering" at a local church.

We prepared a liturgy, again without religious language, that we hoped would name the pain and fear of the women, help them remember the strength and courage of women together, and find that capacity for corporate solidarity in themselves. Hundreds of women came; most had never entered a church before, and they went away with renewed relationships, courage, and hope. The women who originally approached us were not Christian women; they didn't even know what they were asking for. They knew only that the church ought to be able to provide something they knew they needed.

This is the liturgy that we prepared:

LITURGY FOR THE WOMEN OF BULLI

We Are Not Alone

Informal Welcome

Let Us Remember Who We Are

[lighting of three candles]

Leader: *White is for the dignity of women down the ages,*
               for women who know themselves to be people
               of courage, freedom, and truth,
               for women who stand tall and look life in the face.

All: *We light a white candle for the dignity of women.*

Leader: *Purple is for the suffering of women in every age,*
               for women who are exploited, who are raped,
               who live in fear and bear pain beyond their due.

All: *We light a purple candle for the suffering of women.*

Leader: *Green is for the hope of women,*
               for our determination in the face of discrimination,
               for our capacity to heal each other in the struggle
               and for the energy and strength that we find together
               to create a new world.

All: *We light a green candle for the hope of women.*

Sharing of a Symbol of a Wider Community of Women

[We shared a patchwork quilt made by women at a national conference; it expressed their grief and joy as women.]

Telling the Story

[One woman told an old local story of a mine disaster and the strength of women at that context. Another woman told the story of the current assaults—how the small community was experiencing the impact of the rapist: the fear, the breakdown of ordinary patterns of life and trust.]

Story About the Struggle of a Woman

Naming Our Weeping

Leader: *Where is the pain in our lives?*

[The women were encouraged to name briefly their fears, anger, pain.]

Response: [after each naming]

Leader: *You are not alone.*

All: *We share the tears of every woman.*

Song: "Singing for Our Lives" by Holly Near

Affirming Our Strength

[The women gathered in a circle and linked arms.]

Leader: *Who are the women who have given us strength and*
               courage and created models for our lives?

[The women named those who had been important for them.]

Response: [after a group of names]

Leader: *These women walk with us.*

All: *We do not walk alone.*

Commitment to One Another

[Symbols of unity with other women were distributed—paper flowers made by women in Sydney; messages were attached.]

Leader: *In the face of all our realities:*

All: *We are the people who heal each other,*
                who grow strong together,
                who name the truth,
                who know what it means to live in community,
                who survive and survive well.

Song Of Courage

Blessing

The Christian women present sang a song of blessing with female imagery for God, having asked those gathered to receive it in their own way.]

From this gift of liturgy many people came to a new understanding of the life of the church and the possibilities for more than survival that are offered by its God.

Creating Liturgy

If given the opportunity of creating their own liturgy in response to a church year or other theme, people can experience the profound connection between worship and life.

For example, Christmas can come to life for people as they grapple with what it means for them and write the prayers and affirmations that authentically express that struggle.

One method seems to work well:

1. Gather together a group of five or six people.

2. Decide clearly on the theme of the liturgy—church-year theme, issue, or situation.

3. Identify the elements to be included in the liturgy and place them in order (call to worship, confession, etc.).

4. Take the first main prayer, e.g., confession, and with the theme in mind, ask everyone to brainstorm for words, phrases, or images. Do the same thing with the other main prayers or segments of the liturgy. Write the ideas on newsprint, for all to see and take notes.

5. Invite each member of the group to accept responsibility for using the ideas presented for one particular part of the liturgy and shaping them into a prayer, affirmation of faith, etc., Ask them to bring their written contributions back to the next group meeting.

6. At the next meeting, the group reads aloud the proposed pieces of liturgy, hones them, and moves toward putting things together.

7. The group comes up with ideas for making the theme come to life with symbols, music, dance, art, and/or drama.

Using this process, it is amazing how fresh liturgy can become; it moves away from old cliches, allowing people to "own" their worship, even if they only contributed one word or phrase.

Of course, any such activity requires the clergyperson to hand over power to the laity, to release worship into the hands of the people while always holding the final responsibility. Most of us find this hard and threatening, especially those like me for whom the creation of liturgy is our first love. But if we will let go, even a little, experience tells me that our special gifts will be affirmed over and over again; the people of God will worship in Spirit and in truth in a new way.

CHAPTER III

Carrying the Word into the River

The Word is given to and received by the people in many ways: in the lived-out Gospel of action and caring, in personal relationships, in the Sacraments. In this chapter I will concentrate on preaching as the vehicle for the Word. In the Protestant tradition, in particular, we have held a strong belief in this method of communicating the Word; even the architecture of our churches portrays this emphasis. In my original tradition most services ended with the sermon, a closing hymn, and benediction; the people left worship with the sermon still ringing in their ears. I recall that when arguing for the sermon to be brought forward in the liturgy, I was countered with the argument that the people might forget the sermon if it was followed by the prayers and the offering.

In many traditions, a candidate's capacity to preach well is a primary requirement for ordination. Sometimes this gift has to be recognizable even before clerical training. It's no wonder that many of us move into parish ministry seeing preaching as one of the special gifts we will bring to the people. Every week, sometimes more than once a week, we are expected to prepare a new and important delivery of the Word.

Training for ordination normally includes lots of Bible study, theology, ethics, metaphysics, and other elements meant to help us with this work. We try to collect significant Bible commentaries and resource books to keep us up with biblical scholarship; we save stories, poems, and illustrations in hope that one day they will be useful to us in our sermon preparation. Most of us will also receive training in the structure and delivery of a sermon.

I recently sat next to a newly ordained minister who had all these things at his fingertips, and yet he anxiously asked, "Dorothy, have you done your sermon for this week?"

I said, "Matthew, it's only Tuesday. I've read the lectionary passages, but I haven't done the work yet."

He said, "But I'm worried about what I can say. What do you think the main points are?" I gave him a few thoughts, and then he said, "Where do you *really* get your sermons from?"

I realized that seminaries and theological colleges can give us all the information and references in the world, but in the end they can't actually give us our sermons—the Word for the people. I knew exactly what Matthew was asking. He was facing the fact that the Word is more than information, more than clever illustrations. It is a powerful and costly delivery of the life-changing Gospel.

Having said that, I need to acknowledge that there are different traditions. In some churches the sermon is understood as something not unlike a lecture on a biblical passage—primarily a teaching rite. In other churches the sermon is called a homily and is a usually brief advising of the people in relation to a Bible passage. In some churches the Word emanates primarily from the preacher; that is, the preacher, through prayer and spiritual leading, determines the main theme of the sermon and finds a Bible passage to suit that theme. In other traditions a lectionary is used and the preacher is expected to draw the particular Word for the day from the set passages. In my tradition we are encouraged to use a lectionary, and I find this an essential discipline. Whatever the style or tradition of preaching, I would like to offer some thoughts on where sermons come from and what preaching is about.

Bringing the Gospel to the Congregation

A basic requirement for a preacher in our parish is that he or she be capable of bringing the Gospel to the congregation. Delivering the Gospel is not to be confused with telling people the meaning of a Bible passage. A biblical scholar can competently take you through a Bible passage but still leave you without the Gospel. Indeed, a preacher can leave everyone in despair or leave everyone feeling guilty and accused. How many times have you sat in a pew and listened as a preacher used the pulpit-platform to tell you in the congregation exactly what the preacher always wanted to tell the congregation about itself—the failings and shortcomings? How many times have you sat in a pew and heard more information than you wanted to hear and nothing that remotely connected with your life? How many times have you come away from some superbly presented bit of literature—beautiful in itself—with nothing that touched you, nothing of significance to carry into your life? How many times have you sat in a pew and suddenly realized that you had switched off some time ago and didn't have the faintest idea of what had been said? Of course no preacher can avoid losing people some of the time, nor can we always be relevant for every listener. But we can always at least invite people to hear and be open to the Gospel.

Though each of us follows a unique path to understanding the Gospel, as preachers we have the responsibility of grappling with Scripture until we reach the point at which we say "Aha!" and feel a sense of urgency for the service, knowing we will take the people toward that Gospel. There comes a moment when the Bible passage opens up before you; it becomes the Good News for you in a fresh way and you feel an inner imperative to communicate that experience. This enlightenment does not necessarily arise from a personal mood that is sympathetic to finding the Gospel. On the contrary, some of my most significant sermons have been birthed as I have sat looking at the Bible with a sense of emptiness, tiredness, and discouragement.

I recall once facing the Beatitudes at a point when my own personal life was in considerable disarray. Indeed, I was close to breaking. I sat with my head in my hands despairing that I would ever again be the vehicle of Good News. As I bent my head, I heard the Christ say, "Blessed are the poor in spirit." For the first time I understood the overwhelming power of the Beatitudes and saw that they are not really rules by which we earn the blessing of God. On the contrary, if we are poor in spirit, we may be given the kingdom of heaven as a gift. I experienced, as one who was poor in spirit, the gracious blessing of a kindly God pouring healing balm over my being.

At other times I have wished to be rid of the lectionary passage because I have found it hard to accept or understand. I have been engaged, like Jacob, in a life and death struggle with the passage, trying to control it until finally it asserts its power over me and turns into a hard-won Gospel. Then there have been times when I have come to sermon preparation with nothing to give because I have given my energy and time priority to people and situations from which I could not turn away. All I could do was go through the basic preparation and have faith that the gift would be given. In these circumstances I have never been failed by God. I have sometimes gone to bed in the early hours of Sunday morning without a clear sermon and have woken refreshed with the sermon ready in my head, having placed it in the heart of God and waited expectantly. I have received many gifts from God when I least deserved or expected them.

My preparation for a sermon normally involves reading all the passages and then a few modern commentaries on whichever passage I decide is the "lead" passage for the day. I must admit that I rarely get anything much for a sermon from a commentary, yet one still gains something from reading those whom I regard as the technicians of Holy Scripture; they have a capacity to ground the passage in its original context and, I find, keep me within the boundaries of mainstream biblical scholarship. I never reread any previous sermons on the passages—neither mine nor anyone else's. I feel that anything of worth that I "knew" before will be carried on with me; to wrestle with a passage can be done authentically only in and with the present. This does not mean that we cannot receive from the past and from many other people; we do that as we take the biblical witnesses seriously. It means that I always assume that I and we as a congregation have moved on and that the Bible is like a remarkable kaleidoscope; each time you hold it up to your "eye," its pieces shift into a new and special pattern. The pieces are the same but they rearrange themselves so that truth breaks forth in new and surprising ways. Only as you are open to its newness can you draw on the wonder and power of the Bible's eternal truths and great messages in story, poem, art, and expressed wisdom.

After this preliminary preparation, which I normally do early in the week, I "sit" in silence before the passages, letting them turn over inside me throughout the week—a gestation period. I regard this as being a period of prayer, allowing the moving of the Spirit around the passage without my interference with lots of conscious thought.

Later in the week I imagine myself inside the passage experiencing the life and feelings of the people. I concentrate on this especially if the passage doesn't make sense to me. If it doesn't make sense, I presume it's because I haven't been able to get inside the situation. Why did Jesus react the way he did? What issues were people struggling with? What questions were they facing? What were their vested interests? What powers were involved? What were people afraid of? We can never be sure that we have been able to enter any of the situations and feelings accurately, but if we don't try to do this, we end up dealing with abstractions and intellectual theories that make it hard for listeners to connect with the Gospel.

I find that the Bible and its characters have become distanced from most people. We have made it into a sort of "magic" book about unreal and very special people—not ordinary people like us. At a conference I unexpectedly ate breakfast with Ernst Kasemann, a biblical scholar who had written the impressive text on Romans that I was then studying. I remember myself being rather surprised that he looked like everyone else, ate ordinary breakfast food, and could carry on an ordinary superficial conversation.

When we separate the biblical witnesses from their earthly context, we severely reduce their capacity to address us. When I try to imagine what was going on for the people in Scripture, I assume that they were indeed ordinary people like me, with some cultural differences, involved in the same types of human situations that I encounter. After I have tried to respect their situation, I see if I can link their experiences to ours, firstly on a personal and then on a corporate level.

I then ask myself, "What is the Gospel in this passage?" The answer to this is not necessarily an announcement of some clear comfort for us in the struggle. It may involve invoking a great hope that we might be open to completely new things—maybe new ways to love our neighbor, less dependency on the possessions we feel we need, new freedom to forgive, or new willingness to be healed. It always comes in the form of genuinely *good* news, never as a condemnation or a judgment. It always comes in the beautiful form brought to us in the first chapter of Ephesians: "I pray that your inward eyes may be illumined, so that you may know ... the hope to which Christ calls you" (v. 18). It is always offered as an invitation to participate in a great hope.

I work to make that Gospel as clear as I can in all sorts of ways—in different forms of words, poems, and stories: in symbols placed on the communion table; in drama, visual art forms, and music; sometimes in silent reflection when, in community, we wait before God to be given deeper understanding. Yet I always live with the tension of knowing that the most profound things can never be adequately expressed because we cannot capture God or ever give more than glimpses of that mystery of love and truth that is God.

The point at which I am ready to preach is the moment when I, myself, am addressed by the Gospel. It is this sitting under the Gospel myself and therefore existentially staying with the people that protects me from doing other than bringing my witness. A witness always comes through struggling humility and personal thanksgiving. It is always couched in words that reflect the pain, fear, joy, and hope of the journey of all people.

Releasing the Word

I suspect that where we stand to deliver a sermon influences both the way we deliver it and how it is received. I experience preaching from a high pulpit removed from the people quite differently than preaching while standing on the same level as the people. There may be a place for sermons from high pulpits, especially on grand occasions, but I am inclined to think that the distance has an impact on what we say and how we say it. When I stand among people to preach, I can feel their responses to what I am saying. The connectedness is very precious and sometimes costly, as is any disconnectedness; I can clearly feel when I have lost the people. If this happens, more often that not I see that it is when I have become abstract, when I am not quite convinced of what I am saying myself (I usually get very verbose at that point!), or when I clearly know that I am not seen as being engaged in the same life struggle as the people.

Delivering the Word in all its sharpness is a problem only if it seems as though we personally are not pierced by the Word. The temptation to protect the people from the fullness of the Word usually relates to our own fear in some way. The separation that occurs because we are seen as different from the congregation and not really understanding of their struggles has more to do with relationships with the congregation than the content of preaching or the power of the Word. If I feel that separation, I need to look at all our relationships and the perceptions that people have about my humanness or lack of it.

In my first years as parish minister, I found myself in some tension. On the one hand, I believed in releasing the Bible to people in every way. On the other hand, I was afraid that if I handed over the tools of exegesis, of biblical criticism, everyone would know my sermon before I preached it. If we studied the Bible passage for the week, I held back from the discussion—withholding information and generally feeling anxious. This troubled me greatly; during theological training I had felt angry, realizing that I had been denied so much information while faithfully sitting in church pews over nearly half a century. As a minister it took me quite some time to discover that after everyone had rigorously reflected on the biblical witness, I could not only gather up our corporate insights in a way that clarified things, but also bring a fresh Word. I had to learn to trust my own gifts for the ministry of the Word.

I discovered that even a sermon—though spoken with one human voice—can belong to us all and come from us all. My answer to the anxious, newly ordained preacher is that we get most of our sermons from the people themselves—from their lives, their miracles, their struggles, their pain, and their faith. When we preach most effectively we often are preaching not to the people but for them, exercising the special gift of gathering up our corporate experiences and namings of life, placing them in a rigorous encounter with Holy Scripture, and bringing forth the Gospel for their–and our own–new day.

Measuring the Scripture

For me, one of the most inhibiting factors in preaching has been the inadequate way in which most people understand the very nature of the Bible. I do not live in a church tradition that is predominantly fundamentalist or literalist, and yet most of our church members and adherents view the Bible through a lens I can best describe as selective literalism.

My father was ordained in the Methodist tradition more than sixty years ago. Even then our theological colleges had moved well away from literalism, and yet it seems that we have largely failed to give to people a credible way to do the same. Because of this, most people are at the mercy of the difficult questions about the Bible and have an uneasy proof-texting approach to ethics and understanding the Scripture. Because they are afraid to step out of this into what seems like nothingness, they are hard on clergy who try to preach from another position. They get stuck on the line of questioning often presented by literalists, "If you question one text, where does it end?" They hang onto their favorite texts—the ones that confirm their own views—like grim death, being anxiously aware that they have already lost some others along the way.

My colleagues agree that this is a widespread problem. Most of us come out of theological training full of enthusiasm to educate the church and to deliver the Word with real integrity, but then we reel back from attack as people defend their old positions. When I left my training, very good training, I had in my head a general attitude to the Bible and much detailed information about particular passages, but I wasn't sure I could adequately describe my overall view of the Bible in words that lay people could understand. I just hoped that, as they listened week by week and studied the Bible with me, their eyes would open to see the general picture as I had come to see it. But until people *have* that general picture, they are not able to let go of the positions they hold; it all feels very dangerous and they don't know where it might be leading.

I soon realized that I needed to articulate very clearly and sympathetically the position many people were holding. I needed to go a step further and reflect with them about whether they found it to be a good standing place. (Obviously if you are not fundamentalist but serving in a church where fundamentalism is the norm, you and your congregation may simply be incompatible. However, most of us are not in this situation.) If you clearly describe the selective literalism that most people hold, they will admit that it feels as if they are holding onto planks of a rapidly sinking raft. They have grown up thinking that you should read the Bible as though it were a set of true-for-all-time rules for life and faith. As they live longer and explore the Bible more, it becomes clear that some of the Bible may be put aside as inappropriate for our day and that other parts are rather troubling. They don't really think, for example, that women are unclean when they menstruate or that slaves should obey their masters. They are troubled about descriptions of an apparently violent and warlike God and note that there are two quite different creation stories at the beginning of Genesis. These things they can put aside most of the time, but others they can't. Somehow it seems particularly dangerous to meddle with the biblical witnesses when it comes close to home, when their lives can be related quite directly to texts.

For example, we have very few proponents of slavery these days. Since discussion on the merits of slavery is virtually dead, ignoring Paul's texts on slavery feels quite comfortable to most people. On the other hand, because discussion regarding the ordination of women is current and passionate, many people feel quite alarmed at the thought of ignoring Paul's texts on the subservience of women, even though some of them are right alongside the texts on slavery. The problem at least in part arises because we still talk about "ignoring" or putting aside various texts as though we were gradually eliminating bits of the Bible. It is no wonder that people have a feeling the the Bible is being stripped until it may one day disappear altogether. Is anything sacred?

I find it helpful to describe my own view of Scripture as follows: I believe the Bible is an amazing and vivid account of people's experience of God over thousands of years. It is primarily an account of God's faithfulness in the face of messy humanness. It doesn't matter that these hundreds of accounts don't always add up or that they come out of many different contexts and cultures. On the contrary, the miracle is that as we read the biblical witnesses, if we take a wide and sweeping view, we can see the great themes about who God is and who we are in relation to God. We can see that God is at the center of all creation, and we can write our own creation stories alongside the biblical witnesses. We can see the eternal love, grace, energy, and healing that is God. At the center of the Bible for Christians is the witness to the life and death of Jesus Christ in the gospels.

Every text in Scripture must be measured against the gospels and the great themes about the nature of God that run powerfully through the Bible as a whole. So we are not dropping texts at our own convenience but requiring each witness to bow to the central revelation of God in Jesus Christ and the overall wisdom of the combined experience of the centuries of inspired biblical witnesses. That is, after all, the very process that the church has used through the centuries to build up a body of truth. We do not allow one witness of faith to determine the faith of the whole. We listen; we struggle together; we ask ourselves whether the insight has arisen elsewhere; we test it against our understanding of God and life, and we incorporate the view or throw it away according to its consistency with everything else we understand. In all of this we look for the inspiration of the Holy Spirit, just as the church did when it selected the books that became the canon of the Bible.

Of course there will be passionate engagements as we discuss this because we only "see through a glass darkly" (1 Cor. 13:12 KJV). But we don't need to apologize for the process itself or feel anxious that we have before us in the Bible a delicate book that could be destroyed by our questions.

As bearers of the Word, we have a grave responsibility to help people toward a credible and defendable understanding of the Bible, the church, and life. If we don't, they will cluster in ghettos and attack us when we open up new possibilities. Their faith will become like a precarious house made of a pack of cards. They will live forever with the fear that if someone pulls out one card, the whole structure, their faith, will collapse; they will crucify the person who attempts to pull out the card.

The Responsibility of Bearing the Word

To bring the Word to the people is to breathe life into the vision of the promised land—the state of the reign of God—and the experience of life in the river. As the Spirit works through us as we proclaim the Word, people see in a fresh way the possibility of their relationship with God. They join us, having decided that we are the people who can best accompany them on the next part of their journey. They will stay with us only if together we have created a Body of Christ that feels, bears, and celebrates real life. They will usually be very long suffering in this if we have convinced them from the beginning that we are all failing, all betraying, all human; that we grieve as we go, pick ourselves up as we receive from God the gift of a new day, and go on in new hope.

As bearers of the Word who take our stand in the river of life, we have the responsibility and privilege to watch for opportunities to name the Word for the people. As their faith runs low and the way becomes hard, we are the bearers of hope—not a trite and easily offered hope. The hope we offer will be received when it is born of our own blood, sweat, and tears, when it comes from the toughness and frailty of our real struggles. Often its smallness will add to its credibility—like the small and vulnerable child of Bethlehem, the small, delicate light of the incarnation of the Christ.

CHAPTER IV

Caring for One Another as the River Sweeps On

What is the pastoral task of the church?

It is easy and probably true to say that the pastoral task of the church is holistic; there is nothing in the developing of whole and healed persons that is not our task. Yet, if we are to be good stewards of our time and energy and at least try to ensure that the unique gifts of the church are offered, we may need to work out priorities and acknowledge that people other than clergy have a substantial role to play.

Many excellent therapists, for example, are much better trained than most clergy to do psychotherapy. Medical professionals are trained to care for the body, and paramedical people can help people relax physically through different forms of massage and manipulation. There are fitness experts and countless other forms of restoration and recreation services offered for the health and well-being of people. Sometimes it may be most appropriate for us to respond to people who come to us seeking material help. But, even in this field, we are usually less well equipped and resourced than social workers in various governmental or private agencies.

So, while we may need to be the front-line person in assessing the nature of a person's need, we often serve as a referral service. And then we stand wondering whether there is nothing more significant that we can and should offer. I see this feeling especially in clergy who wish to move away from viewing their primary role as "savers of souls" in the narrow sense. They—we—do not want to hand people over to other agencies of care and consequently be seen as the ones who offer the "spiritual" help.

Offering a Healthy World View

Perhaps we need to develop a new confidence and clarity in perceiving and offering the very special gifts that we have. If we reflect on those in trauma with whom we are working, it may become apparent that while the trauma in itself is difficult for people to handle, the shattering of the person's world view is ultimately more serious. Most of us are still living out some variation of a very childish and primitive view of reality: If we are good we will be rewarded, and if we are bad we will be punished.

Someone living out this unsustainable view of reality will be deeply offended and disintegrated when trouble comes. Either the God who is trusted to control this neat and ordered life has been overcome by greater forces or that God is angry—but why? On top of the pain of the traumatic situation itself, life has become hostile, meaningless, and confused. Feeling betrayed, the person's faith—whether in God or in the meaning of life—breaks down.

At this stage some people leave the church and some come to us for answers. And here we are faced with whether or not we have worked out a viable world view for ourselves. Will we reaffirm the old view in the person—of good and bad, reward and punishment—or will we stay with them while they rebuild their world view? Will we point to some possibilities for their reflection?

If we reinforce their old view of reality, we leave them carrying the burden for everything that happens—they must have caused it—a view that relates to the simple understandings of a child. We not only burden the persons concerned but support them in a mode of thinking that assigns blame to everyone in trouble; we reinforce the view of a God who is no more merciful than an ordinary earthly justice system—indeed probably less merciful. Years later I still remember Christian people responding to the news that a polio vaccination had caused severe brain damage in our eldest son. I heard comments like, "What could you have done to bring this on your son?"

If we affirm this interpretation of life, we encourage people to believe that everything is based on a system of reward and punishment, to search for the "sinner" who caused the trouble. As they do this they often condemn innocent people and create a harsh God for themselves and others.

This understanding of reality also supports a view of God that interprets any good fortune as a blessing of God. It is easy for the rich to be seen as the righteous and the poor to be seen as the sinners. Because it cannot really make any sense on a universal front, it requires the person to interpret life dishonestly to sustain the "rules" or to deny reality on a wide front.

Most people would like to have a viable view of life from which they can defend their faith and feel secure. We can, of course, simply hand people a mystery for a world view—the God who has some deeper and unknowable purpose for all our suffering, or the God who is testing us in some obscure way, preparing us for some unknown future. If this is our mode of care, we need to ask ourselves what sort of God we are creating for ourselves and those we serve. What sort of God takes from us our loved child, for example, to serve some mysterious plan? And when can we expect to understand the plan? And what sort of God painfully "tests" us rather than simply inviting us to begin the journey into the tough place for which we are apparently being tested? What good and loving parent would do these things to a beloved child?

So what can we give to confused and shattered people that will equip them for the next step? In my experience, the most fearful thing for people is the darkness, the emptiness, the wilderness of their confusion. As we acknowledge our common journey—that most of us enter into that wilderness at a time of distress and that it is a safe place to be— the solidarity itself is a reassurance. As we name what they are going through—the fact that nothing makes sense anymore or that some people wrongly think that all trouble is punishment—we offer help. After all, in the depths of our soul, most of us, no matter how mature our faith, ask ourselves what we have done to bring trouble on ourselves. Most of us are also quite capable of distinguishing between the legitimate and deserved consequences of our own activities and those undeserved and punishing experiences that life delivers to us.

I think it's doubtful that anyone can actually "teach" people the truth. All we can do for one another is to bear witness to our own understanding of the truth and respectfully allow one another to claim what each sees as truth. This does not mean that there are not clues or that we cannot learn from one another and from bodies of thought that come down to us through the ages. It simply means that, when we care for people or preach to them or live with them, they collect what they believe to be true rather than what we would like them to know.

When people come to a "moment of truth" in their lives, they are sometimes inclined to reach for black and white answers. There will always be someone nearby with ready black and white answers. There may not always be someone ready to take the risk in the relationship and try to help them work toward a more useful and lasting maturity.

A community of faith prepared to ask the hard questions about life and the activity of God within life is not crippled with fear. It is also closely linked with the central tenants of the Christian faith that have to do with life patterns of crucifixion and resurrection. It does not have to try to defend God who is supposed to be administering a universe run on a system something like that of Western civil justice! Life is simply not like that, and the sooner we admit that the easier life becomes.

As we face the hard questions about God and human suffering, we are likely to grow genuinely respectful of the pain of other people—to sit in respectful silence, grief, and compassion before it instead of pouring out inappropriate, trite "answers." We become part of a community of people who rest securely in the love and good that is at the center of everything but does not save us from struggle and pain; the love is simply found at the center of our pain and walks with us as we go.

As we face the hard questions, we begin to understand prayer as the joining of our love, health, and healing energy with that which belongs to God. We know that we can share this life force in faith with results that are always creative but never predictable because God is God and we are not. We can see ourselves as part of a creation that could not be built on rewards and punishments; if it were, we would all be "good" and live in a bargaining relationship with God. We would not choose the relationship out of love but because of the rewards it would bring to us.

As we face the hard questions, we can see the wonder, the passion, and the rigor of it all as something that is part of the very fullness of life—something that has the capacity to create strong, free, self-respecting people who can choose to relate to God or not.

In the end, clergy must model for all people the Good News that, in spite of inequitable beginnings, life circumstances, support systems, and contexts, we need never bow to the view that our lives are predetermined or defined by others. We need never ultimately live like victims. Unless we are too young or too severely disabled, we have choices. For some the choices will be far harder to make than for others; this needs to be recognized with compassion, respect, and extra support. There are always choices for individuals, for systems and institutions, and for the Body of Christ itself.

As a pastor I need to carry with me the passionate love that does not protect people from those choices and that gives evidence of my own hard choices. Real love is not sentimental and wishy-washy. It is tough; it invites people to face reality; it gently and respectfully holds them while they take the next step forward in life. It acknowledges that almost all growth toward life is accompanied by pain and assures people that the journey is ultimately safe as God in Jesus Christ accompanies our every step.

Who Am I as the Pastor?

The answer to this question very radically determines the whole process of our caring. It also determines the nature of the relationship we have with the people we are pastoring when they are no longer in need of our particular care. It may also affect the effectiveness of the corporate life of the congregation and its capacity to care for itself.

It took me a number of years to work out an answer to this question. I certainly did not come out of my training for ministry with any sort of clarity. Indeed, I was carrying with me a rather anxious feeling that I had to be all things to all people and that I would be a failure if I did not have most of the answers to their needs and questions. Of course God was going to play some part in all this—mostly when I came to the end of my resources.

Most other "helping professions" have a much clearer picture of their role as they work with people. They have fixed appointments for which people pay by the hour. When the hour is over, as a rule, the relationship is expected to end. Clients come expecting to receive a particular expertise within a reasonably narrow boundary. They are not interested in the personal life of the "expert," and nothing much is jeopardized if they don't like that person; they just go elsewhere.

On the other hand, we as clergy are expected to work on a very wide front of caring. We are usually not paid directly by the person concerned, although, if a parishioner, the person may expect unlimited amounts of time and attention in "exchange" for the offering given at worship. Our personal lives—or even those of our spouses or children—

may well affect the pastoral relationship, and we are expected to peer relationship with the "client" as a potential or actual member of the Body of Christ. All this adds up to a very difficult relationship. I believe it means that we need to be a great deal more honest in discussing the dilemmas involved.

Let me contribute to the public discussion my understanding of myself in the pastoral role at this point in my ministry: When I pastor a person, I am not sitting there trying to think of solutions to that person's problems. I am watching, listening, and feeling very carefully and respectfully for the signs of Christ within him or her—strengths of courage, freedom, capacities to survive, insights into truth, love for self and others, honesty, and any signs of hope, however dim. My task is to point to any of that which I can see.

I can do that in a special way because, as a person of faith, I believe that all people have within them unique ways of connecting with God and restoring their own energies for survival. If I watch and listen, I can help people discover their own "themes," the particular ways in which their spirits are renewed so that they can recognize and develop their own capacity for survival. When people are sharing their lives with me, I see myself as a companion on the way. When they have expressed something of this grief or despair, I can ask, "How have you survived in all this?" I then help them reflect on the answer. With some help, people can usually begin to see that they have within them amazing capacities for survival. They also see that what works for others need not be the answer for them.

For example, some people restore themselves by sitting in silence and stillness under a tree on a high mountain. Others restore themselves by intense activity—spring cleaning the house or swimming one hundred laps of a swimming pool. Some people gain energy and courage by walking in crowded places and others by returning to a cozy womblike spot.

Sometimes I ask groups to do the following exercise as a way of discovering each person's survival spirituality. The same questions can be asked in a pastoral relationship.

- Remember your most vivid experience of the presence of God— a moment of awe, wonder, personal energy or power, an intense experience of something beyond yourself. Where were you? What were you doing?

— What is your favorite text or poem?

— What is your favorite hymn?

— If you were asked to bring an object that most reminded you of God, what would it be? (If there is preparation time, people can be asked to bring the actual objects.)

— If you had to bring an object that reminded you of yourself, what would it be?

As a pastor I am the journey companion who reminds people of their own resources and encourages them to develop them more intentionally. If I am a good companion, I am continually teaching people that life is intended to be lived corporately—that the resources for survival are not given to us individually but together. Indeed, they are given to the whole creation. When community breaks down and we do not care for one another and the whole creation, our capacity for survival and fullness of life is severely reduced. If I give people the impression that their well-being is dependent on my skills or energy, I reduce their chance of understanding that truth. I end up building a congregation that is not really a community of faith but a collection of individuals who are dependent on my care.

This is not to say that I don't have particular gifts as the person who is often the first-line contact and representative of the congregation and its ministry. But if I don't use those gifts to point to the very nature of the Body of Chirst, then I break down the body and probably eventually myself and the people for whom I care. If I am faithful to the idea that we simply need to accompany one another on the journey, I will model relationships that other members of the congregation can follow; they will become more confident in offering their own authentic company without feeling the need to be experts.

I will also be reflecting a sustainable theology in relation to the predominant activity of God in the world. While I would certainly bear witness to gifts of God that involve saving intervention, the primary message we bring to people is the saving power of the company of God along the way. Indeed, this understanding is central to the theology of the incarnate God.

The Pastor and Authority

A significant part of the pastoral task for me is connected with my understanding of authority and how the person for whom I am caring understands authority. Many of the people in need of care have a real problem with authority, often having been hurt by some "authority" in their lives. They come to us as the representatives of God—the highest authority they can find. Sometimes they are playing off one God authority against another—shopping around for a kinder God authority or sometimes for a more severe God authority (who will finally punish them enough for their sins so that they can lay them down) or for someone who will with authority remove from them the responsibility for their own lives.

How many pastoral interviews go rather like this? The person asks for just a few minutes with you. He or she tells you something rather minor, all the time watching you carefully to see if you are going to be shocked or disapproving. When you are not, the person gets braver and tells you something more important. Often the story involves events that occurred years ago, some condemnation from an authority figure. At this stage, I usually ask, "Why did you come to me? Is there something you need from me or the church?" The person may tell me that he or she thought I might understand the situation—or be more forgiving or maybe things have changed and there's no longer reason to feel condemned. Then I usually say, "Well, I could tell you that you are indeed forgiven. I could even tell you that you should not have been condemned in the first place. But what happens if tomorrow you pass another church and go to another clergyperson and that person condemns you again?"

After that I go on to help the person name the problem: Over all these years she or he has clung to the hope of a God who was more gracious than the one that was once offered. Deep down that person was really honoring a higher authority than the one she or he was respecting. The ideal way to live is to connect ourselves with groups of people who honestly test out with one another their own perceptions about God and life and who learn in that context to respect their own inner authority so that they are not destroyed by false authorities.

Pastoring in My Humanness

Sometimes as a pastor I can point parishioners to resources and resource
people. Sometimes I am given insights into possibilities that people have
not considered before. As I offer these things I can say that I am simply
recycling the gifts of the community in which I move. Sometimes I can
be quite open and vulnerable in identifying with people's pain from the
reality of my own life experiences. This needs to be done appropriately
of course. Most people in trouble do not actually want to know the details of my life. What I am at pains to convey is that I am engaged in the
same human struggle as they are.

As I sit with people, I do not sit there simply as a mind, soul, and
heart. I am also a sexual body, a whole person present. As I enter into
intimate relationships with people, often with ones who are not currently
engaged in fulfilling intimate relationships, I may become aware of
sexual feelings running between us.

If the feelings are primarily mine, I can say to myself, "Yes, I am a
sexual being and have sexual feelings for this person. I am in a professional relationship. It is important to be conscious of these feelings in
the context of my grave pastoral and ethical responsibilities." I find such
self-honesty and deliberate awareness necessary in monitoring myself
and choosing to be appropriately controlled.

If I become aware of possible feelings from the other person, I often
say something like, "I sometimes have the feeling that you might be
feeling attracted to me. If that's just my imagination, no worries. If it's
not, I just want you to know that such feelings often arise when people
enter into an intimate pastoral relationship. I am not uncomfortable with
your feelings, but I want you to know that I don't want to encourage
them. I am honored that you like me."

I find that people are relieved when feelings are named in a non-
threatening way and are usually released from hopes and fantasies. Of
course if the level of sexual feeling on either side continues to be inappropriate, I refer the person to someone else. In saying all this, I recognize that the main issue for most clergy is not about avoiding compro-
mising situations behind closed doors (never close the door when you are
counseling a person of the other sex); it is about being impeccably responsible at each point in any relationship.

At times, my resources for providing pastoral care will run dry.

Journeying with people, even if it is not as stressful as finding answers
for people or creating emotional and spiritual dependencies, uses a great
deal of energy. It is costly because we grieve with the grieving and
suffer with the suffering. I have learned that part of the peer relationship
with those I pastor is to respond authentically to that reality of ordinary
humanness. People need to know that I get tired like everyone else.
They need to see, lived out, the respect that we are each called to have
for ourselves. They need to see that, although God can give gifts of extra
energy and wisdom for critical situations, we are not called to live driv-
en, "superhuman" lives with apparently inexhaustible energy. We are
rather called to work, play, rest, celebrate, be messy, be well organized,
be reflective, and be active in a balanced harmony of life.

I have found that if I do not respect my own need for rest and recreation, I end up subtly rejecting people because I do not want to be
with them. I even find myself making less than truthful excuses for not
seeing them rather than honestly asking for their understanding of my
needs. On the other hand, I have found that people who thought they had
nothing to give to anyone can find a new respect for themselves if I ask
them to give me rest and recreation by postponing their need for my
company.

Do You Want to Be Healed?

Of course there will always be people who try to manipulate their way
past our decisions about how much time we have to give them. Despite
my attempts at keeping reasonable boundaries, I sometimes fail, though
always with regret, as I know that I am not helping the person concerned
by bowing to such manipulations.

Every pastor knows some people whose need is insatiable. Their
lives have become defined by their perception of themselves as needy,
and they no longer know how to relate to others in any other way. Sometimes a history of tragedy, injustice, and damage in the lives of people
like this makes it hard to imagine that they can be other than dependent.
Often, when they lift their heads and appear to be coping better with life,
their "care givers" are so relieved that they reduce the level of care,
which makes the dependent person panic. The needy person often feels
that if he or she became less dependent, all care and attention would be
withdrawn, even if this isn't true.

while, as pastor I have the responsibility to ask the question,
to be healed?" If this is asked in love, the honest answer
...ved with grace. We all have emotional wounds that we do
not want healed. Maybe we want to stay angry until someone confesses
and asks our forgiveness. Maybe we want to stay hurt until someone
recognizes the extent of our pain. What if you ask the question, "Do you
want to be healed?" and the answer is no? Affirm the honesty and stand
by with care. The question invites a person to be aware that, at this point
in time, she or he is choosing to say, "I am not ready to be healed,"
instead of blaming other people for the dysfunction. I also find that
when I discuss with people their fear of withdrawal of care or their fear
of wholeness itself, the struggles become easier. Sometimes people can't
imagine what it would be like to be seen as a freer member of the community with the accompanying self-respect and affirmation. They need
to be reassured that such a transition, though not easy, is worth the
struggle.

Underpinning all that I do pastorally is the absolute conviction that
God is at the bottom of every abyss, is the oasis in the desert, the light in
the darkness that is never extinguished, and the waiting meaning in the
nothingness. If I cannot bear confident witness to this, I need to retire for
a while and recover my faith. I may articulate the reality of doubt, alone-
ness, fear, and emptiness that people feel as they experience the apparent
absence of God, but my sacred calling is to announce the Good News
that ultimately life is stronger than death.

I never cease to wonder at the power of this faith. To my joy I discover in my own life and in the lives of others that everything else can be
stripped away; we can be betrayed, stripped of all manner of things we
think we depend on, destroyed and grieved almost to the point of death,
but the great hope of the ultimate victory of God and the company of
God in everything can still save us. This truth, paradoxically, can become even more powerful if we don't pretend that there is more than that
hope to offer when there isn't. The base line for me as pastor is authenticity, and when people experience my authenticity connecting with
theirs, we are able to live creatively together with God and one another.

CHAPTER V

Standing in the River of the World

The prophetic ministry clearly belongs to the whole church. Though some individuals may be recognized as having prophetic gifts that lead the people of God forward, I don't see the prophetic ministry as an optional extra for the church—as though we have to wait for a person with particular gifts to arrive before anything happens. The prophetic ministry of the church is not, of course, about foreseeing the future in "fortuneteller" fashion—nor do many of us in the biblical tradition regard it as that. It has to do with the sacred calling of the people of God to so love the world in which we live that we always call it, and ourselves, to a new and great hope. Sometimes this will sound like a warning for the future; sometimes it will be an honest accounting of what we see in the present.

In the environment in which I work I do not see the accusing style of prophetic activity as being appropriate. Nor do I believe that we are called to be intentional martyrs of our day. What model did Christ give us? I am not convinced that Jesus decided that he would die, then organized his life around that. He decided to love and live more fully than anyone had ever done. In reality, those who do that usually have to be stopped because they model a life of such passion that they threaten every power of death among us.

If you look at the prophetic ministry institutionally, perhaps it is possible to see it like this: In every institution there are fundamentalists who believe they "know" the truth; they become the people of the law as they try to insist that everyone else bows to their views of eternal "truth." Then there is a large group of people who adhere to that institution and are just "there." They may find it hard to explain why they are there but they stay, many with considerable faithfulness. Then there are always the rebels who fly off the edge of institutions. Though they sometimes challenge the things the institutions stand for, they end up in some wilderness by themselves.

Then there are the people I see as the prophets. They love the institution and have some credibility within it, but they sit on its margins with one foot treading a new path. They model what it means to be "the way," often allowing their bodies to be used as the pathway to positive, corporate change. Some never see the new day because they care enough to become the way. Some do see the newness, but they carry the price within their persons.

The prophetic community of faith tries, in a fragile, human way, to model the new order, the reign of God. In its life and its witness to truth, it points to new possibilities, even when it falls short of those possibilities itself. When it does fall short, its credibility stands because its authentic confession is evident; it has been struggling with the same issues as everybody else.

Daring to Hope

The shocking thing about a prophetic ministry is that it dares to hope. Indeed, in my experience, to announce hope is very threatening to the powers of evil. Martin Luther King once said that to occupy the ground of justice is to expose the nature and reality of the powers of injustice. Parts of the church and the community will see this occupation as aggression; they will do extraordinary things to reclaim the ground. As I mentioned earlier, our congregation experienced two years of attack and harassment from a neo-Nazi group because we dared, in the most modest way, to indicate our belief that we could live together as a multicultural society. We dared to set up an antiracist graffiti group that wiped out or covered over racist graffiti in our area, and we hosted Archbishop Desmond Tutu of South Africa.

Though we were doing pathetically little, in some way we were apparently imaging a hope that threatened those who did not want that hope created.

In going through this experience, we learned many things about sustaining a prophetic ministry. We learned that a large part of the wider community longs for a church that will stand for justice and truth. In a society that has the reputation for being hostile to the church, we found people from all walks of life fighting for us and putting pressure on the state minister for police and the police commissioner to give us protection. On one occasion we had members of the media organizing a rally with the slogan "If the police won't protect this church, we will." Even in a society where the church seems to have little credibility, people still hope that the church will be what it should be.

We learned that prophetic action involves never seeing oneself as the victim but as always taking the initiative in the power of the Holy Spirit. For a long time we chose to remain silent under attack so as not to give publicity and encouragement to a racist group. Then we chose the moment to expose the group, feeling the community had a right to know its own realities and make its response. We saw that to remain silent was to participate in the negative activity. So we wrote an open letter in the public press: No matter what the group did to us, we would not be moved from our view that all people were equal and beautiful creations of God and to be welcomed in our country. When they increased the attacks on us, we called the police to do what they were supposed to do—protect citizens from unlawful attack. Then we called the community at large to join with us in a celebration of the unity of all humankind.

We prayed, and many people prayed for us. They, and we, were surprised when our prayers were answered. We were enabled to live without dread and to sustain our normal lifestyles rather than bow to the threats around us; we gained rather than lost members. The powers of darkness had less power than the powers of light. They could hurt us physically and damage our property, but they could not destroy our spirit, and our life blossomed and increased every day. We were tired but not stressed. With far greater clarity, we suddenly knew what we were meant to be, and many trivial things fell away from our corporate life.

This experience and others convinced me that if the church is to have a prophetic ministry, we must reflect on the theology that underpins it and develop a spirituality that sustains it. It is easy to become "messianic" in struggles for the reign of God. If you really, deep down, believe that you are going to bring in that reign, it is all too easy to become arrogant and self-righteous or to end up in despair. What needs to be firmly in place is the clear conviction that God brings in the new day; we are only humble but unique participants in a great continuum of human endeavor alongside the God who has already won the victory.

We need to have an eternal view of life so we can sustain the struggle through a powerful view of a reign of God that is both now and not yet—a view that stretches confidently to an "end-time" that belongs to God but in which we share, as we live as though it is already here. In this way we begin to develop a mature prophetic ministry that includes a theology of liberation sustained by a theology of exile.

The Process of Change

Prophetic ministry is often perceived to be most impressive when it is very attacking. I would challenge that understanding of effective prophetic ministry. Christians who genuinely care about change must surely work to recognize how people actually change. Most of the evidence indicates that people do not often change because they are attacked or pressured. Nor do they often change because they are given lots of information about something. Commitment to the status quo has far more substantial underpinnings than information. It is a good exercise for members of any group to remember times of personal change and analyze how it came about.

Most people come to see a process for change that started with a new awareness that invoked grief, unease, anger, or pain. If this emotion can be shared in a safe relationship—an empathic relationship where fear, anxiety, and anger can be expressed and accepted—change can be contemplated—in time. Paradoxically, it is usually easier to find the courage or strength to change if the supportive person or group shares mutual humanness—fear and anxiety akin to the one contemplating change. The initial awareness—the conception—is the least part of the process. It's followed by a period of nurturing or gestation, and, finally, the loved and supported person or group is able to bring the change to birth.

The role of the clergy in this is often to model the change process in an overt, personal way. It is also to create the best climate for change—that is, (1) to articulate the fears and griefs of the people in a way that signals that they are appropriate and acceptable and (2) to sustain the Word of hope and the gentle encouragement needed for the nurturing process. Then the clergy need to help celebrate or mark the moment of personal or corporate change so that it becomes a salvation memory.

Transforming the Institutional Climate

In most Western-culture countries, the church has focused on individual change rather than institutional change, though the biblical witnesses make it clear that salvation is to come to the whole creation. Systemic evil usually has a far greater capacity for death and destruction than personal sins, and we are clearly called to direct the prophetic ministry toward that dimension of our life together.

To be serious about a prophetic ministry requires us to be sophisticated in analyzing the nature of power—how it works and where it lies— and where better to explore that than in the church itself? Why not encourage people to attempt the transformation of their own church environment as a rehearsal for the work of change in the world outside the church? Of course we will be no more popular working against negative power in the church than anywhere else. The powers close at hand are very difficult to deal with, especially if they wear the faces of friends. And unstructured power is as hard to shift as structured power because few people will admit that it exists.

Many available resources can help facilitate a serious structural analysis of power, a congregational group may benefit greatly from walking through such an exercise. Most churches resist such work as it seems unpleasantly like politicking. And yet, without at least some minimal consciousness raising in this area, it is hard for people to understand why efforts for change don't work.

The Nature of Positive Power

Alongside this, clergy can help people reflect on the very nature of positive power. Most of us learn about this the hard way. I certainly did. As a younger, very shy woman, I occasionally managed to find my voice in the councils of the church because I passionately believed in some cause. With dry mouth and trembling knees, I would rise to my feet and say a few words for peace or for women or for something I cared about very

deeply. Every effort like this cost me dearly and was an act of faith.
After a while it became a little easier. I could think on my feet in de-
bates, and the church began to see me as a token woman to put on committees and councils. I was rising in the system, and, without realizing
what was happening, I was changing.

After some years, I was representing the church at national and international levels. I was active in a political party and the women's
movement and felt a call to the ordained ministry. I entered a theological
college and began my journey toward ordination. At this stage I became
aware of a grave misgiving about ordination. Thinking it had to do with
concern about joining what might be seen as a hierarchy, I made the rounds
of the theological college questioning whether anybody ought to be
ordained. Then, through other people, God gave me a series of challenges.

At a meeting of our synod, two young ministers came up to me.
"Dorothy, we need a 'heavy' to help us get this resolution through. Will
you help us?" The principal of the theological college introduced me to
a few people as "one of the most powerful women in the church." When
I protested, he said, "Well, I see you demolishing chairpersons of pres-
byteries in debate all the time." When I spoke, women would come up to
me and say things like, "Well, it's easy for you, Dorothy, but it's much
harder for ordinary people like us." Dimly, I became aware that some
sort of power was accruing to my person. It was almost to the stage
where I could say something stupid and others would not dare to challenge me.

All this disturbed me, but worse was to come. Deep down, I knew
that sometimes when I spoke or acted I measured my words for effect; I
was increasingly conscious of whether or not I would gain approval. I
imagined myself in new positions of power. When someone said, "You
are mellowing in your old age, Dorothy," I told myself that I was just
becoming more effective for the cause.

Then I did something I had never done before. I had by now learned
how systems work, especially church systems, but my role had simply
been to "needle" away on committees, saying what I believed, gaining
support by persuasion. This time I and a friend decided to organize
ourselves. We lobbied; we set someone up to get control for us in a
particular situation. Because we were inexperienced, we were not very
subtle. At the critical meeting, we saw the light of recognition dawn in
the eyes of our opponents. We won, yet we knew we had lost. Having

entered the power game, we were less powerful—less dangerous—than before. Why? Because we were playing the same game as everyone else. I remember my friend wryly saying to me, "Those who live by the sword will die by the sword, Dorothy."

At this stage, I placed myself under spiritual direction, an act that was a significant part of my journey away from bad power. Being prepared to confess my need of direction I opened myself to the possibility of change. This was the beginning of a long and painful process, yet every time I separated myself from an old power, I received the gift of freedom, energy, courage, and new power. In the end, I decided against ordination and announced my decision to my family, friends, and teachers.

Having made my decision, I had a sense of absolute desolation. I went into a favorite church of another denomination (ironically one that refuses to ordain women) for the lunchtime Eucharist. At the communion rail, still feeling full of grief, I knelt to receive the elements. As the chalice was placed in my hands, I saw a light around it. The priest took the chalice and moved on, but I saw with wonder that the light stayed in my open hands. With the most profound joy I knew that God had graciously returned to me the gift of my ordination. I saw that the issue had not been ordination itself but my own dealings with destructive power. I was now less dangerous to myself and the church because I had seen the difference between *power over* and *power for* other people, though I still struggle with the issue and probably will for the rest of my life.

If we are to release the prophetic ministry of the church, we must courageously and honestly struggle with the people of God in their understanding of the nature of negative and positive power. We should never be afraid of power. If the world is to be delivered into the reign of God, we cannot lay aside our responsibility to grapple with power in all its forms. If we see clearly our own patterns of power, we will more ably interpret power in other people and in systems of oppression.

We must do this within the church, which has more capacity to be demonic than other institutions. I say this because any institution that claims to represent the mind and life of God moves beyond offering people a simple opinion about reality. It carries with it the gravest and most sacred trust. When it violates that trust, it has the capacity for the most destructive, demonic power over people because, in their trust, they believe that they are being addressed by the mind and life of God.

So we are called to be the people who dare to engage with all power in the most intentional, honest, prayerful, and gracious struggle. And one of the best safeguards against a congregation becoming embroiled in negative power is the consistent inclusion of a body of marginalized people. Because they have little to lose and have stripped away many of the pretensions and inhibitions most of us carry around with us, they are likely to keep us all more honest. Power is always most safely exercised from the margins.

CHAPTER VI

Planning the Route

Planning our life together as we swim the river or walk against and with its currents can be moving, celebratory, and fun.

Over the years I've worked with or observed many congregations that never spend time together to plan their corporate journey. I've noted characteristics of these churches: There's an uneasy or guilty feeling that they should be doing more or better, coupled with a rebelliousness against church committees that are always asking things of them. When they are challenged in sermons and study groups to become the people who live out the mission of God, they feel powerless and inadequate. Some people respond to all this by giving or withholding money depending on whether they approve or disapprove of decisions being made.

They also fall into relational patterns that include frequent discussion about "some people" who are doing all the work and others who are slacking around the place. They often feel that if only some expert could be brought in, things would be better. Or if only the pastor would leave. . . This sets up a dreadful relationship of blame and counter blame because nothing seems to be happening or working.

Of course some congregations appear to be happily and comfortably maintaining their own life like a social club without ever questioning that anything should be different. Try to challenge the lifeless status quo, and you usually see one of three responses. Some are not really as complacent as they look. Like the rich young ruler, they long to know the secret of eternal life, but when they are invited to move into the journey, into the flowing waters, they turn their faces sadly away. (Sometimes you can see this literally.) Then there are those who still hear the call of God very deep down and remember their decision not to answer that call. They punish anybody who repeats the call and often try to destroy the messenger. The third group can listen to the call and not even realize that it applies to them at all. They will warmly congratulate you on your fine and inspiring sermon, encourage you to keep up the good work, and sometimes offer to pray for you and your work.

When I moved into ordained ministry, I found a congregation with a great capacity to move beyond all this because they had a great tradition called the parish planning day. Originally held once a quarter, it was changed to twice a year (due to increased congregational membership) and is now the annual parish planning day. The creative processes involved in this day hold the key to why this parish survived the most difficult periods in its life and thrives with a good degree of fulfillment.

Parish Planning Day

This is what we do:

We send a personal letter to every member and friend of the congregation. Here we emphasize the importance of the day and encourage every woman, man, and child to be there to share ideas and directions for our life together in the coming year. We indicate that all are welcome whether they have been in the parish for two weeks or twenty years. Indeed, we point out, this is a good way to understand more about the life and hopes of the parish. We arrange child care from outside the parish so that everyone can come. We outline the process for the day, asking people to commit themselves to a Saturday morning and afternoon together.

In preparing for the event, we type up a summary sheet of last year's planning day to remind us of what we hoped to do and a list of "names of the week" for the past year. (During the morning tea time after our Sunday Service we always "name the week" and write the slogan on a poster to help us remember important events in our life.) These two documents serve as resource sheets distributed as people arrive for the planning day.

On the evening before the event, we decorate the parish hall with posters, with photos that remind us of our community life and the fun it has provided, and with mementos from events that celebrate our year.

The program for the day:

9:30 a.m. Morning tea or coffee

10:00 a.m. A brief opening liturgy (hymn, reading, opening
prayer)

10:10 a.m. We ask each person to write down three things he or
she wants to celebrate from the life of the parish in
the past year and three things about which he or she is
disappointed. If the group numbers less than thirty,
we go around the whole group and share what each
person has written. If the group is bigger, we break
into small groups and bring back the key issues to the
whole group.

Then we have a prayer of assurance of pardon in
relation to all the disappointments and a song of
thanksgiving for all the celebrations.

When done acceptingly and honestly this part of
the morning helps people bring to the group the
realities that they experience as pain and helps those
in a negative mood remember that there are things to
be celebrated. It also gives a picture of the real
diversity that is present. We always emphasize that
this is a respectful hearing of people and is not open
for discussion.

11:30 a.m. Dreams and visions: We ask everyone to write down
three things she or he would like to see happen—
without necessarily feeling personally responsible for
carrying out the dream. All the ideas are then written
on newsprint under category headings, e.g., congregational life, creative use of church property, engagement with the local community, wider church
activities.

(We have recently created and used at this point
subheadings from our ten-year parish vision. See
further on in this chapter.)

12:30 p.m.   All, including the young children, go off to the local park for a picnic lunch.

1:30 p.m.   We invite everyone to join a workshop to work on the list of dream ideas in a category of her or his choice. If there are a large number of ideas under or people around one category, the list and/or people can be subdivided.

Each group takes a list of ideas and follows the following workshop process:

1. Look at the list and decide which idea the group likes best. Have a quick show of hands to decide this, if necessary.

2. Define the idea as a project; describe it clearly.

3. Answer this question: What would stop us from doing this? Write down the answers and decide whether the blocks to action can be overcome. (This question must never be omitted because it holds people to reality—stops them creating fantasies or following what they think they "should" be doing.)

4. What would be the first step to take in carrying out this project?

5. When should we aim to take the first step? Give a fuller time-line if possible.

6. Whom will we ask to do this? An existing group? A new task group? A particular person? (This is also critical so that "they" or "you" are not left to do it.)

7. The group then chooses the second most exciting idea and goes through the process again.

3:00 p.m.   Everyone gathers together and a spokesperson for each group briefly reports on the projects discussed.

Display the write-ups of each project. The large group is asked for any general comments (not debate).

We assure everyone that ideas that have not been worked on by the small groups will be passed on to the appropriate church committees for consideration. Also, all the group project reports will be assigned to the appropriate committees for initiation, coordination, and resourcing (as far as possible).

3:45 p.m.   Closing act of commitment, statement of faith, and the sending forth of the people into the new year of work for the mission of God.

When the appropriate parish bodies have met and reflected on the suggestions from the planning day, a one-page document is drawn up. This lists the parish plan under the headings from the planning day and includes any "given" ongoing activities that don't normally arise as issues on that day. We present the plan for approval at a full meeting of the congregation, following formal reports from the previous year.

The advantages of an open planning session are many. It stops people complaining about others (the mysterious "they") who tell them to do things they don't want to do. It helps a parish assume that things are going to happen—new things. It unloads the disappointments and respects them by giving them a hearing. It reminds people that good things did actually happen. It gives everyone an opportunity to contribute ideas and cuts across old power groupings. It is much harder for the old guard of conservative power brokers to hold sway if they are faced with an enthusiastic group who have even begun to plan how something could be achieved. It uncovers gifts and talents that may not have been recognized. It provides a parish with a plan that it owns, and says it wants to carry out, rather than something somebody thinks it ought to do.

If the "dream" category headings are carefully chosen, the planning session can point out any unhealthy self-preoccupation. When you have a long list of ideas under "congregational life" and almost none under "engagement with the local community," you are somewhat confronted. And the planning day certainly moves people away from the view that "the minister/priest ought to be doing this or that"; it lays the groundwork for a deeper understanding of the nature of the church as a corporate body.

It doesn't really matter if people don't have a complete picture of the reign of God in what they would like to do. It is far better that they start somewhere and find that they can move, achieve even small things, take initiatives. With a plan based on who is there rather than who "ought" to be there, even the most vulnerable group can begin to imagine itself capable of doing something.

Some of the projects that emerge from the planning may be quite modest, but whether the commitment is to disciplined prayer, the watering of the church potplants, or organizing a major effort for change in the local community, it usually moves people on. It is a new beginning.

If people as a group want to do something that seems relatively unimportant, let them do it; maybe they never did anything in a group before. If people decide to tackle something that seems impossible, don't discourage them. Who knows what faith and commitment will achieve? How many moves of the Spirit are stopped by committees of people who have little hope and faith and who say there is no money?

In assessing the plan as it unfolds in action it is important to keep asking questions: Is this project going well? If it is, let us recognize and celebrate the success. Does this project need more resources? How can we guide it to those resources? Does this project need to be respectfully terminated because it isn't working? (It's far better to end something properly rather than to let it die a lingering death.)

Having given all this direction, I must admit that in my time our parish has never gone through this whole process impeccably. We have always fallen down somewhere, particularly in follow-up. Yet, we are absolutely committed to the concept as a way of working together.

Preparing a Ten-Year Vision

Quite apart from annual planning, it is helpful if a parish can work on an overall vision for what it is doing long term. The church needs a sense of identity as the people of God who are at mission. The vision provides this and invites people to name the church as they understand it.

A parishioner skilled and well read in secular models of producing "mission statements" helped us establish the following process, which we found not only significant, but also creative, even fun.

In developing our vision, the key body was our Parish Elders'

Council (the laity and ordained ministers responsible for oversi[
ministry within the parish), but it could be developed by any major
parish committee. We saw the need for a vision statement after the
parish had grown considerably. It was time to ask again, "Who are we?"
and "What do we really think we are doing?

The Committee went through these steps:

1. At an afternoon meeting it identified its values. It answered the
   question, "What do we hold dear about our parish life—its theology,
   ethos, worship, and context?"

2. The list of values was posted in the church for several weeks. The
   congregation was asked to look at it and make any additions or give
   comments.

3. The elders met for another afternoon and made a list of the parish
   "stake-holders"—people or groups the elders believed had a stake in
   our parish life or people they wanted to be impacted by our life.

4. That list was also posted in the church for several weeks. The
   congregation made comments and additions.

5. The elders met again. Each was asked to write a brief mission statement for the parish—not longer than one short paragraph. We all
   placed our statements on the table and walked around and read
   everyone else's statement. We were asked to set aside the original
   statement we had written and write another one. After reading one
   another's second drafts, we repeated the process a third time. Then
   the council nominated three of its members to go away and draft *the*
   mission statement, which was posted and agreed to unanimously.

6. The draft mission statement was placed on the communion table for
   everyone to read and comment on. There being no negative comments, the mission statement was unanimously accepted by the
   congregation.

7. The elders met again and took each phrase of the mission statement
   as a heading. For each heading they said, "therefore we will . . ."

Under each heading we developed a list of general goals. We used these goals as category headings for the next parish planning day.

8.   We made a banner of the mission statement and hung it in the church after a special service of commitment.

Our mission statement

In our humanness and frailty, we seek to embody the presence of God through celebration and sharing our experience of loving community. Through commitment and faith, we will live in the struggle to restore right relationships in the whole of creation, moving towards a city and a world which reflects the justice of God, the compassion of Christ, and the freedom and peace of the Holy Spirit.

Our mission statement expanded into goals

1.   As a loving community we will relate to one another and to new-comers in a caring way.

2.   We will care for people even if we don't agree with them.

3.   We will create a community that affirms the gifts that each person brings and provides opportunities for the development and expression of those gifts.

4.   We will help people who are hurt to find healings.

5.   We will be a community that reflects human diversity.

6.   We will welcome the stimulation of diverse ideas and experiences.

7.   We will aim for a lifestyle of sharing resources.

8.   We will equip people to act in pursuit of peace and justice in domestic, neighborhood, and global spheres.

9.   We will support people to act in the pursuit of peace and justice in domestic, neighborhood, and global spheres.

10. We will take a stand as a parish on issues of peace, justice, and freedom and act in solidarity with victims of injustice.

11. We will join with environmentally aware people to protect and conserve the resources of the earth.

12. We will live together in the struggle for truth by overcoming our prejudices, developing understanding by openness to the Word and the Spirit.

13. In all that we do we will be aware of our humanness, frailty, and freedom to fail, recognizing our dependence on the love of God, Grace of Jesus Christ, and the power and leading of the Holy Spirit.

14. In all of this we will celebrate the hopes and joys of life.

To plan and produce visions is not an end in itself, but if a congregation has lost its sense of dreaming and even forgotten that action is involved in being Christian, then a process like this does become significant. I am told that death by drowning is rather painless. Once people move beyond the initial moment of panic, the next phase is all too pleasant and relaxing. If we stand still in the river of life and faith, it is entirely possible to move into the euphoria of drowning without even realizing what is happening.

This sort of death is particularly easy for churches that are not dependent on their own giving income for survival. If you have significant income from property, for example, it is all too easy to avoid the life and death questions. You can decrease in numbers, even push out new and disturbing elements who might try to enter, and just go on comfortably dying.

Modeling the Reign of God

A critical factor in bringing people back into the journey is to invite them into a planning and envisioning process that feels good and encouraging rather than accusing and full of "we should be doing this—or that." Sometimes the God we represent in planning is frighteningly relentless.

We might well ask ourselves why God gave us gifts—beautiful beaches to play on, waves to ride on, mountains to climb on, trees to sit under, rainbow shoelaces for our shoes (a recent gift for me), wonderful imaginations, laughter, and a million other ways of delighting in rest and recreation—if that God did not want us to enjoy those things. Planning can always represent that gracious and playful God, acknowledge our tiredness, and lead us forward into a life that is lived out in truth and abundance. Anything less is not a modeling of the reign of God.

People also respond to calls for action more readily if they feel that they have opportunity to relate their concerns authentically and trustingly. The best planning processes in the world become empty abstractions if people are not in relationship with one another and don't feel that their real views are taken seriously. There is a sense in which people can only plan for themselves, not for others. That means the church is always the actual people present offering who they are; it is not some imaginary model of who *ought* to be there. So the question "What would you like to see happen?" becomes critical, moving people beyond unreal expectations and unhealthy pressures.

CHAPTER VII

Hidden Dangers in the River and Hints for Survival

As clergy we are in a dangerous profession. If we don't see it as dangerous, I believe we are in even more grave danger.

The Risks

There is a risk in seeing ourselves as stepping into the river of life ahead of the people: We are tempted to see ourselves as "special." Any leadership role carries that temptation, but to be seen as representing God is to be tempted to see ourselves as God. Then if people around us are disrespectful, we can be tempted to do things that are spectacluar and ego-restoring.

The whole priestly tradition teaches particular respect for the clergy as the source of significant salvation. We are "there" to meet everybody's needs; is that not what we are paid to do? In many cases we are people whose personalities feed on being needed. We are the ones who are regularly up front with all eyes upon us (except those whom we put to sleep). We speak and most people in our congregations listen. We are the ones who must visit people or they don't feel visited, even if they have had twenty lay callers. I don't need to lengthen this list.

Even in this day when clergy are less likely than in the past to be seen as community leaders, the people we serve still feed our egos day after day, week after week.

The Seductions and Temptations

We stand in grave danger of being egocentric and the slope is so slippery. We are seduced and easily rationalize ourselves by appealing to
the very nature of our role. I mean, can we help it if all these people
admire us? Is it not good and right for them to respect God's priests and
ministers? Would it not be worse if they didn't?

When we are honest with ourselves, those of us who are highly articulate, even charismatic, in our ministry style, know our power. Which
of us is not aware of the responses of the people as we speak and preach?
Now and again I can "hear" my own voice as I preach; it is a moment of
unhealthy separation as I stand outside myself and listen as though my
performance has some value in itself. I become a performer, and I am
playing the audience.

By nature of our helping profession, we are at times necessarily in
the company of people who sustain their own lives by being dependent
on us. No matter how professional we are in dismantling this for the
other person's sake, we would not be human if we did not occasionally
find other people's dependency gratifying.

Then, of course, there is the pressure on all clergy to be models of
the perfect person—the dehumanized one who does not experience life
like others, with all its failure and general messiness. Because there will
always be some people who need us to be like this and who punish us if
we appear otherwise, we will always be tempted to present ourselves as
superhuman. Sometimes we will actually believe it.

The Life and Death Struggle

I have discussed earlier the potential damage to the church community if
we become enmeshed in all these hazards to our wholeness. The battle is
hard. Sometimes it feels as if the risks in confronting these hazards are
less than the risks faced in succumbing to their power. After all, there
are rewards in living out the clergy role as many people perceive it ought
to be. We would, in fact, be standing secure in what is now a great
tradition!

But, dear sisters and brothers, what will become of us and those who
follow us if we do not at last face these tough issues and face them together? What will happen to us if we lay down true life in order to meet

the expectations of other people? And how will we stand with the people in the river if we cannot courageously grapple with these hidden hazards? Is this not one of those occasions when we profoundly understand what it means to lay down our lives for Christ's sake and find our true selves?

We are indeed engaged in a passionate life and death struggle, and the demonic principalities and powers against us can come in the guise of friends.

How Can We Defend Ourselves and Stay Human?

Sometimes the costs to our own personal relationships bring us to our senses. Though congregations may encourage us on false and destructive paths, those who have a personal investment in our humanness can call us away from the dangers or at least protest about who we have become. When we won't stop to see what is happening to us, they will sometimes risk challenging our cleverly disguised, inflated egos that defend ourselves against our own pain and fear and emptiness, clad with a shell of cliches about life and faith. I know we can become like that because I have been there. The "clever" bit is reflected in memories of my attempts to "play" at therapy—pretending to be honest and real with my counselor but actually laying out carefully calculated vulnerabilities. It's a terrible thing when one can play at being vulnerable.

We Need Honest Families and Friends

I find infinite value in friends who have little or nothing to do with the church. I hate it when one special friend who sits on the edges of the church will say—just when I think I have preached my finest sermon— "What on earth were you talking about today? And you put on that voice again, too." But I know I dare not ignore her. I know that she is not afraid of me in any sense, nor does she depend on my approval or have any extraordinary respect for me or the church. Moving among people who have no particular interest in my role as clergyperson (who even think it odd that anyone would want to be such a thing!) is very healthy. The things that tend to gather around you in a church setting disappear, and you are no longer supported in seeing yourself as "special." This is quite a good litmus test. If you feel unreal and alienated in this company, you still have important work ahead of you, as this is the real world.

We all need family and friends who will keep reminding us what abundant life is like. Life is not abundant if you are engrossed in work and the needs of other people. Life is not abundant if you rarely have fun, laugh at yourself, express yourself in creativity, look at the wonders around you, or simply stop and do "nothing." Life is not abundant if you dare not stop for fear you might discover your own emptiness and depression. Life is not abundant—it is not even your life at all—if it is consistently defined by others and their expectations of you.

Finding Our Own Way to Healing and Recreation

We each have to find a personalized style of recreation. Sometimes I go on brief retreats. When I arrive the spiritual director always tells me that for the first forty-eight hours I am to do nothing but relax and allow one question to surface in my consciousness: What is the deepest desire of my heart? I know to expect this, and on the way to the retreat house I always believe that I already know the answer to the question. I am always wrong.

I also always travel toward the retreat thinking that I am going there because I am up to the neck with everyone else's pain. I always find that the pain inside me is really my own, and I'm forced to face the full extent of the danger in which I have placed myself and those I serve. I marvel at my capacity to be so separated from my own feelings, and I wonder what I have been doing to myself and those around me.

For recreation and healing I also do sculpture. For about half the year I attend a weekly class. In quiet community with a small group of students, most of whom I have never met before, I express myself in clay. The experience of putting my hands in the earthy clay is therapeutic in itself. The choice of subject is an important part of my process. The one time I lost interest in what I was doing, I realized I had chosen a subject from my head rather than my heart. I've titled my pieces: "Weeping Woman," "Militant Madonna," and more recently "A Study on Rape."

Into each of these pieces I poured my heart feelings, which changed from week to week. Though I don't totally understand the process, the translation of my experiences of life into works of art is a symbol for me. Each piece takes a long time, partly because the process of sculpting and casting is time consuming and partly because my teacher refuses to let me settle for doing less than my best.

Why was this insistence of his difficult for me? I had to face the fact that I had settled into a lifestyle of rapidly doing many things reasonably well. Actually I had gone a little further than that. I had moved into a pattern: Working hard against deadlines, I would say to myself, "That is good enough. It will do. Of course if I had more time, I could do it much better." And other people were saying, "Isn't she marvelous! She does all these things for us. And if she had more time, she could do them even better. We can't criticize anything she does because she is so hard pressed. We should be very grateful that she does them at all." The end result of this style of living has been an addiction to the risk of almost not pulling things off—the adrenalin rush of just getting there, the triumph of managing to do something well enough to gain approval, and being seen as "marvelous." I also, in this, could cleverly avoid ever being accountable to myself or anyone else.

After working a couple of weeks I thought, "That's pretty good. That will do. Aren't I clever? On to the next thing!" My sculpture teacher thought otherwise. Week after week, just as I was thinking how terrific my work was, he would come up to me and say, "Hmmm. We have problems here, don't we? Can you see what I am seeing?" It wasn't just that he was teaching me new things about sculpting. He was pushing me to press through to the point where I would say, "This is the best I can do. I will take the risk of being open to my own assessment and yours." Acknowledging my limits was *such* a risk. But in the end "This is the best I can do" felt not only safe but also deeply satisfying. That great learning was a Gospel experience. As a rule I still live hard up against the deadlines, but I no longer see this as good. And now and again I am prepared to own that I have done my best, which makes me truly accountable.

I find an art form a very helpful way of recreating, debriefing, and healing. In the past, I have found similar expression in writing poetry. You will need to experiment until you find your own way of encountering yourself. Some people find journal writing very therapeutic.

The Reality of Never Being Finished

Apart from the hazards that affect our sense of being, we can add the constant hazard of professional exhaustion—the job's capacity to drain us in body, mind, heart, and soul. This not only burns us out personally, but also burns out our primary relationships as family and friends struggle to compete with the demanding job and its deadening impact on us. I have reflected on the need to see the task as essentially corporate. But even when we try our best to share the work and the responsibility with lay people, it is still an impossible job.

Quite recently, when once again challenged by those closest to me about the regular pattern of exhaustion in my life, I looked carefully at the way I view my job description. The reality is that this job—our job—is never finished. If we do it well, it inevitably expands outwards; it is so multifaceted that we never get the chance to quietly and satisfyingly develop in one or two areas. It constantly presents truly dreadful priority decisions. When someone says, "I am in despair. Please spend time with me," how can we say, "I'm very sorry, I need to spend my afternoon preparing for the next parish meeting or my Sunday sermon"? On top of all these creative activities, we are at the same time supposed to be really hard-headed about the parish finances. While nurturing the strong and free, empowering them to share the task of ministry, we are expected to be the front-line person for all those in crisis.

And then, when we are exhausted from juggling this and all the other complex things set before us, our partners or children have the audacity to expect that they too are due for our care and energy! We can't help feeling that they should just be waiting there for us with the comfort, understanding, and sympathy we need! Even if we are not living stressfully, we are still exhausted.

Where do you start to dig yourself out? Acknowledge to someone other than family that you are tired. It's one step in conveying the fact that you are not superhuman. Then work with others in identifying ways of making your life more manageable. Include members of the parish, so you have their "permission" to take action. At the heart of any action is the "permission" from God to acknowledge that you are not able to save the world; you are free to leave things undone and people's needs unmet. This is a hard view to hold that may require being inaccessible for whatever amount of time is necessary for survival. It also means discovering how best and where best to rest.

Finding Rest

I feel as though I am resting and caring for myself if I say, "I am leaving here (where I work) and going out." Even during the ordinary work day, I find it infinitely more restoring to go next door for coffee than to sit in my office and drink coffee. If I drive up the mountains on my day off, I feel much more cared for than if I try to rest at home. It's as though I am rewarding myself for working so hard and taking my tiredness seriously.

Late in life I am being taught by others how to play a little—to dance, to party, to dress up for fun games, to feast, to picnic, to laugh, to enter the absurd, to swim in the surf, to lie in the sun. And I've learned to relax as I listen to the conversation of others. I can rest at a point where I might previously have felt impelled to point out that someone was incorrect. A friend once said to me, "Do you always have to be right?" I immediately thought, "Yes, I do." But she has taught me that I can live, even thrive, without that level of arrogance and false responsibility for every conversation. Many things simply don't matter, and it's quite possible to leave them be.

There's nothing wrong with resting by totally escaping for a time, as long as it doesn't escalate to a long-term escape from facing the realities of life that need to be resolved. I love reading mystery novels myself. We all need to block off everything for some of the time.

Apart from the legitimate responses of those closest to me, the most accurate monitor of my well-being is my body. The young among us may be able to close off the messages their bodies give—for a while. But once past forty-five years, most of our bodies refuse to be overridden. I value a doctor like mine who, when I describe some complaint that I am sure has some clear physical origin, will sit, give me a meaningful look, and say, "So . . . tell me about your life at the moment, Dorothy."

At one time I tried hard to convince myself that I was not a person who had stress-related physical symptoms. When the doctor said to me, "You have had a migraine. Are you under stress?" I took offense. I told myself I was *not* the sort of person who gets migraines. Interestingly, I didn't get any more migraines. Instead, I got carpal tunnel syndrome, which was also stress related. When I said to my body, "You are not the sort of person who gets carpal tunnel syndrome," it stopped evidencing that symptom and went on to another. Fortunately my doctor patiently challenged me about my lifestyle.

In the end I not only faced with reality the level of stress under which I was living, but also began, for the first time in my life, to love my body, care for it more, and listen more respectfully to its messages. I even decided to cherish my body a little, with massages, soothing oils, and perfumes. Though I am improving, I still have a long way to go, being rooted in a strong family heritage of ignoring bodily messages, being stoic about pain, and not "indulging oneself." At my age I can see the benefits of cooperating with one's body and caring for it beyond a maintenance mode.

In all this I have discovered that to be kind to oneself, to love one-self, is, as Jesus reminded us, part of the path to loving one's neighbor.

And Is It Worth It?

I celebrate my calling to the ordained ministry.

I have never known such love in my life—the love of people for me, my love for them. The rewards—and challenges—are great. So few professions carry such variety, such unpredictability, such a breath-taking honor of accompanying other people through experiences of both joy and pain.

As we take our stand in the river, we may well wonder what lies ahead for us each day and each year. In our hands lie the bread and the wine and the water of the grace of baptism. When these precious ele-ments were placed in my hands on the day of my ordination, I won-dered if I would ever be worthy of carrying them. But as I broke the bread and offered the wine, I realized that the life I held would never be dependent on me or the strength or worthiness of my hands. A presence was always there in once-offered grace and freedom; it was simply named by me and claimed in thanksgiving by the people of God.

I wondered if I could ever bear the consistent responsibility of bearing the Word to the people, but I have found that it has come to me over and over again as gracious gift waiting to be shared.

I wondered if a person like me could ever be used by God for the task of ordained ministry, and I have found that God can use the most ordinary people, like me, in all sorts of surprising ways. In the power of the Spirit, I—we—can overcome many inadequacies.

If I had my life to live over again, I would not hesitate to respond

again to the same call. The waters of the journey may be deep and sometimes very rough, but nothing for me comes anywhere near the excite-
ment, the passion, and the dreams involved in doing what I do. Every
morning I wake with a sense of gladness that God has called me to this
particular ministry.

NOTES

NOTES

The Alban Institute:
an invitation to membership

The Alban Institute, begun in 1979, believes that the congregation is essential to the task of equipping the people of God to minister in the church and the world. A multi-denominational membership organization, the Institute provides on-site training, educational programs, consulting, research, and publishing for hundreds of churches across the country.

The Alban Institute invites you to be a member of this partnership of laity, clergy, and executives—a partnership that brings together people who are raising important questions about congregational life and people who are trying new solutions, making new discoveries, finding a new way of getting clear about the task of ministry. The Institute exists to provide you with the kinds of information and resources you need to support your ministries.

Join us now and enjoy these benefits:

Congregations, The Alban Journal, a highly respected journal published six times a year, to keep you up to date on current issues and trends.

Inside Information, Alban's quarterly newsletter, keeps you informed about research and other happenings around Alban. Available to members only.

Publications Discounts:

☐ 15% for Individual, Retired Clergy, and Seminarian Members
☐ 25% for Congregational Members
☐ 40% for Judicatory and Seminary Executive Members

Discounts on Training and Education Events

Write our Membership Department at the address below or call us at (202) 244-7320 for more information about how to join The Alban Institute's growing membership, particularly about Congregational Membership in which 12 designated persons receive all benefits of membership.

The Alban Institute, Inc.
4125 Nebraska Avenue, NW
Washington, DC 20016

Dorothy McRae-McMahon was born in Tasmania in 1934 into a Methodist clergy family. She has worked as a preschool teacher, full-time mother, and on the staff of the New South Wales Ecumenical Council. She was ordained in 1982 and has since then ministered with the people of Pitt Street Uniting Church in the center of the city of Sydney.

For the last six years she has chaired the National Mission and Evangelism Committee of the National Assembly of the Uniting Church in Australia.

She spent four years on the General Committee of the Christian Conference of Asia, was a member of the Worship Committee for the 6th Assembly of the World Council of Churches, and is presently on the Steering Committee of the newly formed International Association of Urban Mission.

She has received a number of awards from the community: Jubilee Medal from Queen Elizabeth for work with women in N.S.W., 1977; Australian Government Peace Award, 1986; and Australian Human Rights Medal, 1988. In 1992, Dorothy McRae-McMahon received an Honourary Doctorate of Letters from Macquarie University in Sydney for her contribution to the life of the community.

"Dorothy McRae-McMahon's small book, *Being Clergy, Staying Human: Taking Our Stand in the River* is an immensely readable reflection of the wisdom and creativity of the author. Writing from the perspective of the Uniting Church in Australia, the book is a compendium of sage advice about how to stay healthy in the ordained ministry, creative ideas for services of worship that touch the lives of all sorts and conditions of people, and a theology of ministry that embodies both mutuality and servanthood. The strength of the book, however, lies not only in the wisdom it offers, but also in the warmth and humanity of a remarkable pastor who has a unique ability to make her life and deep spirituality available to others."

> **James C. Fenhagen**
> *The Cornerstone Project*
> *815 Second Avenue*
> *New York, NY 10017*

"I have worshipped at Pitt Street Uniting Church, Sydney, Australia, and spent time with the congregation. It is an honest, open, caring community, energized by its specific stands on issues of justice. It is not 'Dorothy's church,' centered on its minister. She moves among the congregation as a minister aiming to be human rather than heroic, trying to give leadership and be vulnerable. Her book gives fresh vision about ordained ministry, and gives me heart. It shows the unexpected cleansing/healing power of imaginative ritual—for individuals, churches, and communities. It encourages us to give up the 'old power' of power-over, and try on the new garments of power-with and power-for. And it shows how planning can aid congregational empowerment. I have been helped by, and warmly commend it."

> **Brian Wren**
> *Minister, Theologian, Hymn-Writer*

"What a wonderfully refreshing book on pastoral theology!

"By honesty, vulnerably, openness, courage and recreative escapes, Dorothy is leading her congregation into life's currents not by walking on the water, but in it with the people. The chapters on worship liturgies and sacraments (ch. 2 and 6) alone, made this a very special book for me."

> **Raymond J. Bakke**
> *Executive Director*
> *International Urban Associates*
> *Chicago, Illinois*

Resources for people who care about congregations.

ISBN 156699-056-

HOORAY!

_____

can read this book!

US $3.99 / $5.25 CAN

ISBN 978-0-06-162629-6

www.harpercollinschildrens.com

BOOK NEWS, GAMES, CONTESTS, AND MORE

9 780061 626296

50399

S